COUNTY COUNCIL OF DURHAM

### COUNTY LIBRARY

The latest date entered on the date label or card is the date by which book must be returned, and fines will be charged if the book is kept after this date.

FORGOTTEN RAILWAYS:
Volume 8

# South Wales

JAMES PAGE

DAVID ST JOHN THOMAS
DAVID & CHARLES

# To Ann

FORGOTTEN RAILWAYS
Edited by Allan Patmore

The master volume, *Forgotten Railways* by H. P. White, in a larger format, has now also been published.

British Library of Cataloguing in Publication Data
Page, James H. R.
  South Wales. – 2nd ed. – (Forgotten
  railways; v. 8).
  1. Railway services. Disused routes – South
Wales
  I. Title   II. Series
  385'.9429'4
  ISBN 0-946537-44-5

Typeset by Typesetters (Birmingham) Ltd,
Smethwick, West Midlands
and printed in Great Britain
by Redwood Burn Limited, Trowbridge
for David St John Thomas

Distributed by David & Charles Publishers plc
Brunel House   Newton Abbot   Devon

Distributed in the United States of America
by David & Charles Inc
North Pomfret   Vermont 05053   USA

# Contents

# Acknowledgements

I am grateful to many friends and the staff of numerous organisations who have generously given help and provided information. To Lt Col R. H. Edwards for his kindness in giving much valuable information relating to the Taff Vale Railway from his personal family records; to G. Davies and R. Arnold of the Cynon Valley Library, Aberdare, for access to their collection of documents and photographs; and to British Rail, Western Region, for permission to quote from their publications.

I am also indebted to Messrs J. Aitchison, R. Bebb, H. Phillips, R. Taylor, E. Vest, The Gwili Railway Co, the staff of the National Museum of Wales (Maritime & Industrial Museums at Cardiff and Swansea), the Central Reference Library Cardiff, Merthyr Library, Carmarthen Library, and the Chief Technical Officer Merthyr Council, who each assisted in many ways and provided local information. I would also like to thank Mrs G. Anderson for typing the manuscript.

Finally, to my wife and family goes my gratitude for their support and encouragement, and a constant supply of coffee.

JHRP

Machen, Mid Glamorgan                                                    1988

## AUTHOR'S NOTE

Where appropriate throughout this book I have used the old county names. In addition I have also used placename spellings as they appeared in contemporary railway timetables and other publications, and which may therefore differ slightly from current spelling. The maps show the pre-grouping ownerships of lines, but stations opened after 1922, when the GWR absorbed many of the local railways in South Wales, are also shown.

Note: The description of an old railway route does not imply that there is a public right of way along it, and readers must obtain permission to enter private land.

# CHAPTER 1

# The South Wales Scene

STILL ALIVE IN A CHANGING WORLD

When I wrote the first edition of this book I had at an early stage a pleasant surprise, for much more of the railway system remained than I had originally thought. Rural lines certainly had been annihilated, and we were the poorer for this, for much fine scenery was now beyond the traveller's view. The industrial areas, in particular the region known as 'The Valleys', had fared much better, for while 'inter-valley' lines had largely disappeared, only one major valley, the Afan, had at that time lost its railway completely.

Much has happened however in the years since 1979, for as is well known colliery closures have been sweeping, with the inevitable effects upon the rail network. These changes have raised the problem of how to present this new information. This has been overcome by including, immediately in front of an updated and enlarged gazetteer, what might be termed a 'Postscript' in which will be found a resumé of the lines that have closed in the last decade, joining those of earlier years amongst the 'forgotten railways' of South Wales.

But to me the closed lines of South Wales will never be 'forgotten railways'; my memories of them are too many. I shall always remember their stirring sights; a 56xx 0–6–2T labouring noisily up to Dowlais, and 42xx 2–8–0Ts slowly descending Glyn Neath bank, (or were they being pushed by their loads?). I shall always remember the variety; like standing on Barry Town station wondering where the ugly 0–8–0, standing alongside more familiar types, had come from, (it was an ex-LNWR G2 on an excursion from Tredegar). Finally, I shall always remember the everyday sights of a busy railway going about its normal duties.

The railway arrived in South Wales as the successor to canal and tramroad, being a more efficient method of transport for the ironworks of the North Glamorganshire and North Monmouthshire regions. The railway grew with them and then outgrew them. As the old ironworks closed, either because of technological change or defeated by the economies of hauling imported iron ore from the coast, export coal became the principal traffic. This was soon supplemented by steel products, from the few works that had weathered the technological change, or moved to the coast. With this traffic the railway system continued to flourish. An entertaining by-product of this growth was that in industrial South Wales each main valley, or group of valleys, had its own individual railway company. This was also true of the larger ports, and all, whether of valley or port, were quite adept at poaching in their neighbours' territory. Also certain national railway companies had the same idea and many valleys, before the 1923 grouping were tapped by the Great Western, London & North Western, and Midland Railway Companies.

This great railway expansion had a further effect. Spurred on by the successes in industrial areas, rural border regions, the uplands around Brecon, and West Wales were opened up. Financially they were never viable, or perhaps only for a short period. Time has dealt harshly with them, the border regions and uplands having been completely stripped of their railway systems, while in West Wales little remains except the lines to Fishguard, and the oil terminals at Milford Haven.

Time has dealt a little less harshly with the industrial areas. Certainly by comparison with the past they are but pale shadows. They have suffered from the death of the export coal trade and the colliery closures. Bus and car have robbed them of much passenger traffic. Inter-city services still survive, but such commuter traffic that remains is heavily subsidised.

Todays destinations of the remaining freight traffic have, however, caused marked changes in the direction of their flow. Traditionally the railways' wealth was made by the export of coal and iron and steel products, resulting broadly in a north-south traffic flow. Now there is a considerable flow of oil and related products to other regions of Great Britain, together with coal and steel products, although some of the latter are exported. General imports also sustain a flow of traffic which is balanced by products for overseas from other industrial centres. Thus a broad east-west traffic flow has now been established, replacing the traditional traffic patterns.

Before proceeding further, a popular misconception should be corrected. It is widely supposed that the industrial 'Valleys' constitute South Wales in its entirety. Nothing could be further from the truth. The 'Valleys' are contained in an area of North West Monmouthshire, North Glamorganshire, and a small part of South East Carmarthenshire. The remainder of these counties are either urban or rural. In addition the surrounding counties of Breconshire, Cardiganshire and Pembrokeshire are almost entirely, and beautifully, rural; there are scenic delights here to equal any in more well-known tourist regions of Great Britain. The east of the region contains quiet wooded valleys of blissful peacefulness. South Glamorganshire is a delight of low rolling hills, and the far west has beautiful regions fully on a par with Devon or Cornwall, and is tragically underrated. Finally the uplands of Breconshire have a grandeur the equal of Exmoor or Dartmoor.

At the grouping South Wales handed over no fewer than 16 railway companies to the Great Western system. Add to this the numerous private lines in the area, the LNWR and MR interests, and one has a density of railways unequalled anywhere in the country. Because of this one time density, to describe every defunct line in South and West Wales would be a monumental task. Thus with a few noteworthy exceptions, minor valley feeder lines, industrial lines, and railways built solely for dock use have been omitted.

In their heyday South Wales industrial railways conveniently grouped themselves about the exits, either by sea or land, from the Principality, with the rural lines centring on the market towns, such as Monmouth or Brecon. The exits chosen largely determined the character of the lines. Those that headed for the ports were in general blessed with gradients that fell towards the sea, and with a length of run rarely exceeding 25 miles. This resulted in quite heavy trains only requiring tank locomotives of moderate size and strength. This, in turn, coupled with the requirement of only moderate speeds, led to the widespread use of the 0–6–2T type. Such locomotives were characterised by a high adhesion weight, required for starting and stopping heavy loads, and a sufficiently short wheelbase to negotiate all but the sharpest curves.

The lines that headed for the Principality's land gateways to England usually had much more difficult problems to contend with. Gradients were rarely favourable; in fact the routes resembled switchbacks while the length of haul to any destination was considerably longer. This resulted in the use of much more powerful locomotives usually of the tender type, and led the GWR and LNWR to develop specific locomotive types for this traffic, eg Churchward's outside-frame 2–6–0 Aberdare class of 1902, and Bowen–Cooke's 0–8–4T of 1923. The Midland merely drafted in its ubiquitous 0–6–0s.

Those quiet lines which ran to the market towns of Monmouthshire, Breconshire and Carmarthenshire were for years the haunt of small tank locomotives. Some came new to these lines, but the majority came only to work out their last years in semi-retirement. Older rolling stock was the order of the day for passengers, and everything had that timeless character so well known and loved, of the country branch line.

The rolling stock of all the companies was once easily identifiable by the liveries. Those of the English companies are too well-known to require description, but the smaller Welsh ones are worth recording. The Barry Railway used a dark lake for locomotives and passenger stock. Black was the preferred locomotive colour of the Rhondda & Swansea Bay, Cardiff, and Taff Vale Railway Companies. The latter once used red-and-chocolate, and for many years its passenger stock was painted chocolate-and-white. The Rhymney Railway was indecisive, its locomotives were Brunswick green, not unlike the GWR, but its coaching stock was dark lake, like its neighbour the Barry. The accolade for colour must go to the Brecon & Merthyr, for it is reputed at one stage to have had brick-red locomotives and purple coaching stock. Even goods trains were provided with colour by the colliery wagons, for it was a feature of the South Wales coal traffic that it was nearly all carried in privately-owned wagons. Each coal company had a distinctive livery, adding a splash of colour even to the humble coal trains.

As well as individuality in motive power and livery each company was distinct in its architecture. To be charitable to some, it is only fair to describe their styles as 'functional'. Many used locally quarried stone for their buildings, but any 'sameness' brought about by using a common source of materials was offset by the decorative styles used for window and door surrounds, or the style of roofs and chimneys. The B&M preferred to dress many of its buildings in a skim of concrete, notable exceptions being Brecon and Rhiwderin stations. This produced an overall drabness about its architecture which separated this line from its neighbours.

As elsewhere, rural stations had facilities equal to, if not better than, their industrial counterparts. Monmouth had more than ample provision for its passenger traffic, which was never intense. It had two platforms, a long single-storey booking office and waiting rooms, a beautifully ornate awning with distinctive barge boards, and a covered footbridge. Such a provision of facilities, coupled to tasteful design, only occurred in industrial areas where rival companies, at the turn of the century, competed for commuter traffic. The best example was on the Taff Vale Railway's Penarth—Cadoxton branch which was opened in direct competition to the Barry Railway. Facilities of a very high standard were provided, unequalled elsewhere in the area. Although sadly faded and much altered over the years, part of Penarth Town station, now privately owned, still stands as a reminder of the style used on this line.

The GWR also added its distinctive style to the area. Luckily some of the better examples are still with us at Swansea (High Street) and Cardiff (Central). Unfortunately much of this architectural heritage has been destroyed on stations in daily use, by the standard BR brick-and-plastic waiting room building which makes no concessions in style or material to its surroundings. The LNWR and MR have left nothing of architectural note, except possibly the LNWR at Tredegar. Here still stands the remains of a nicely balanced single-storey red brick station building, of a style superior to anything in the neighbourhood.

For some of the companies much of the civil engineering was in general unspectacular, unless they were forced to choose routes that did not follow the valley floor. If they cut across valleys, went over their heads, pierced the mountains that separated them, or were unfortunate in being late arrivals, things were different.

The GWR Pontypool to Neath line crossed four valleys, and in about 12 miles contained three tunnels and three viaducts, including the famous one at Crumlin. The two companies that built from the heads of the valleys to Brecon both suffered throughout their lives with long hard gradients which were nightmares to their locomotive crews. The most spectacular tunnels were on those lines which pierced the mountains. The two most well-known were the Rhondda tunnel by which the R&SB Railway gained access to the Rhondda valley above Treherbert, and the Abercanaid tunnel linking the Taff and Cynon valleys. The Vale of Neath Railway was also notable since on its Dare Valley branch stood two wooden viaducts built by Brunel. They outlived by many years their more famous counterparts in Cornwall, not being dismantled until 1947. Finally there was the latecomer, the Barry Railway, which sought to gain traffic from the valleys north of Cardiff. Being nearly last in the field, all the easy routes had been taken, and to reach its objectives, one branch alone had no fewer than three immense viaducts in the space of about six miles.

Much of the old railway land in rural areas has reverted to nature, though in many places such routes are reasonably easy to follow. In urban and industrial areas the need to bring in new industry has replaced many railway buildings by custom-built trading estates. But possibly the major use for redundant railway land in the narrow and congested industrial valleys has been in road improvement schemes. As a result, many miles of forgotten railways lie beneath present-day roads.

# CHAPTER 2

# Brecon

Four railway companies once served the town of Brecon, although the only tracks that entered the town were those of the Brecon & Merthyr and Neath & Brecon railways, which arrived in 1863 and 1867 respectively. This simple statement says nothing of the bitter battles that took place between these two companies before they settled to peaceful co-existence. Neither does it say anything of the battles between the B&M and the Mid Wales, Hereford, Hay & Brecon, and Midland railways. In fact, the establishment of this rail network was far from simple.

The problems stemmed from the over-ambition of all concerned. The Mid Wales, authorised in 1859 from Llanidloes to Newbridge-on-Wye, sought to extend not only to Brecon but also to Merthyr. The HH&B, also authorised in 1859, antagonised the B&M by purchasing the Hay Railway (a horse-drawn tramway of 1811) over whose southern end the B&M sought access to Brecon. Finally the N&B, whose extension to Brecon was authorised in 1860, spurned connection with the B&M and sought a route to join the HH&B. For years the battles raged until grudgingly each was forced to make concessions in order to survive.

Watching in the wings for much of this period was the Midland Railway, whose ambition was to reach Swansea. Unknowingly the participants in the game of plot and counter-plot, friendship and enmity, amalgamation and disamalgamation were playing right into its hands. Parliamentary and legal battles drained them all financially. The failure of Savin & Ward the contractors in 1866 brought bankruptcy. Additionally, earlier survival had been bought at the expense of extensive mutual running powers agreements (except over the N&B). In 1874 the Midland pounced. It bought the HH&B and used its running powers over the Mid Wales and B&M to reach Brecon. Simultaneously it bought the Swansea Vale Railway (described in Chapter 9). It completed the link to Swansea by using the latter's (unused) running powers over the impoverished N&B, which it obtained on terms highly favourable to itself. Thus ended the battles to give Brecon its railways. All concerned now settled to the difficult task of running their railways through sparsely-populated hill country. That they did so for some 90 years after the Midland's intervention reflects great credit on generations of dedicated railwaymen at all levels.


### North to Brecon

The aim of the Brecon & Merthyr Tydfil Junction Railway, to give it its full title, was to reach the Bristol Channel, which for its very survival was to be an absolute necessity, although this was not realised in its early years. Merely to have joined the two towns of its title would have guaranteed early extinction. Had it sought to reach the sea a decade earlier (it was incorporated in

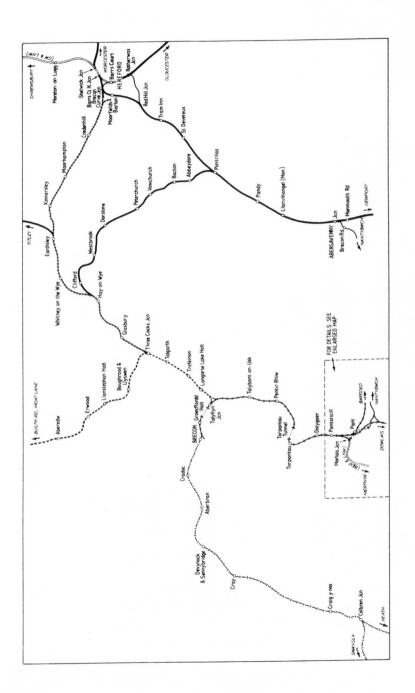

1858) its construction would probably have been a simple matter. In the event, its incorporation heralded a decade of acrimonious fighting to reach the Bristol Channel. Ultimately it achieved its aim, reaching Newport by way of the Rhymney Railway, the rebuilt tramway known as the Rumney Railway and finally the Monmouthshire Railway. The story of this southern extension from Dowlais is told in Chapter 5.

All thoughts of past battles, and the economic knife-edge on which long ago the B&M balanced so often would soon be forgotten as one travelled northwards from Pant. The first two miles fell gently to beyond Ponsticill junction and one quickly left the bleak uplands around Dowlais for the pleasant unspoiled valley of the Taf Fechan. At the foot of this dip came the start of the climb to Torpantau, that isolated station in the treeless mountains, 1312ft above sea level. Before reaching here one had run past the tree-lined Taf Fechan reservoirs near Dolygaer, the haunt of fishermen and yachtsmen. During the last century the reservoir was the venue of an annual regatta, and the line would be almost overwhelmed as the inhabitants of Dowlais and Merthyr flocked to the event. Dolygaer station would almost burst at the seams as visitors from these towns, as well as Brecon and beyond, descended upon it in their thousands. Such frenzied activity is now long forgotten, but Dolygaer is still the centre for the lake's boating and outdoor activities. The section from Pant to Ponsticill once again resounds to the sound of the steam railway, albeit narrow gauge. The Brecon Mountain Railway, opened in 1980, now attracts many tourists to this delightful area to the north of Dowlais. Locomotive stock is of East German and South African origin.

Returning to steam in years past, water would be taken at Torpantau after the stiff climb. Tablets would be exchanged and soon one would be dropping through the dark bore of Torpantau tunnel, once the highest in the United Kingdom. Immediately beyond the incline steepened, and one was on the famous 'helter skelter' descent of the B&M's famous 7-mile bank. To descend or ascend these seven miles of 1 in 38 was an experience never to be forgotten, for added to the thrill of the incline were the fabulous views over the Talybont reservoir, nestling in Glyn Collwyn. Needless to say, runaways were not unknown on this section. Pentir Rhiw station, at which the signalman sold tickets from his box, about halfway down the bank, once served the isolated farms in this valley, many of which were submerged when the reservoir was flooded. At the foot of the bank, 925ft below Torpantau, stood Talybont station. A handsome sandstone building graced the station, and happily it is still in use today. Restored, and only slightly modified, it is used by Newport Education Authority as an outdoor pursuits centre. In summer, where trains once decanted fishermen keen to try their skills on the Usk salmon, it now plays host to a line of colourful tents and upturned canoes.

Back in the hills at the top of the climb, Torpantau has not survived. Only grassy mounds mark the station site at the entrance to a boggy cutting leading to the bricked-up tunnel. The track bed between the platforms is used by farmers for dipping sheep. Gone are the lonely station buildings and the equally lonely signalbox. Here in the early days of the company, the signalmen had to ask for a fireplace to be built in the box. The thought of working at 1300ft in winter without heat is unbelievable. Grudgingly they were given their fireplace. A similar request for sleeping accommodation in the box, since winter snowdrifts often cut Torpantau off from the outside world, was refused.

North of Talybont the Usk was crossed by a lattice girder bridge, traces of whose stonework can still be seen. Beyond lay Tallyllyn, that pleasant station, junction for the Cambrian Railways (the successor to the MWR), lying immediately east of Tallyllyn tunnel. At the time when goods traffic ceased in 1964, passenger services having been withdrawn two years earlier, the tunnel was the oldest in use in the country, being an enlargement of the original tramway tunnel dating from 1816.

Brecon station, opened in 1871, and replacing independent B&M and N&B establishments, was a spacious affair with four platform faces, one of which was an eastward-facing bay. It was dominated by the red brick station building on the northern platform, which was fronted by an awning. It was the headquarters building of the B&M, and also included facilities for the other

companies. Such were the relations between them at this time
that the MWR waited five months before moving in from the
N&B station, while the N&B took no less than three years.

Never a prosperous railway, financial stringency was always in
evidence, and alternative sources of income were always
welcome. The most ingenious was the cutting of grass from the
embankments for sale as hay. The most macabre was the sale of
carcasses of sheep run over by trains, to offset the subsequent
claim of the farmer.

### The Branches

Two branches ran south from this section of the B&M. The first
was at Pant itself, and was a short line to Dowlais (Lloyd Street),
notable only for the size of the embankment built to house the
station and its approaches on the steep hillside below the Ivor
Works. The second was the branch to Merthyr, opened in 1869,
which ran from Ponsticill Junction.

It was a steeply-graded line that descended in a giant sweep
to the floor of the Taff valley. The branch terminated at
Rhydycar junction, south of Merthyr, on the GWR line from
Hirwaun, and thence used that company's High Street station as
its terminus. In 1879 the LNWR reached the branch at Morlais
junction, south of Ponsticill, in its bid to reach Merthyr. By now
the line from there to Rhydycar junction was jointly owned by
these companies, following an agreement reached with the B&M
in consideration of the LNWR abandoning its own independent
branch from Dowlais.

Most noteworthy, and well worth a visit are the two fine stone
built viaducts at Pontsarn and Cefn Coed. The former is tucked
away in the wooded lower reaches of Taf Fechan, but the latter
can be seen from many vantage points, perhaps the best of which
are the grounds of Cyfarthfa Castle. There is a certain irony
here, for the route adopted was selected to placate the Crawshay
family, builders of Cyfarthfa Castle and one of Merthyr's great
Ironmaster families. Original routes proposed were along the
eastern side of the valley passing close to the Crawshay home,
and foundered on their objections. Banishment of the branch to

*Plates 1 and 2.* The Brecon & Merthyr line. *Above:* Ex-GWR 0-6-0PT No 3767 pauses at Bedwas on a Newport–Brecon train in 1959. Note the B & M somersault signal still in use. *Below:* Lonely Torpantau, summit of the line between Brecon and Merthyr, 1312 ft above sea level. (*R.O. Tuck, Glyn Davies*)

*Plates 3 and 4.* In Monmouthshire. *Above*: Symonds Yat in 1958, with ex-GWR 0-4-2T No 1445 propelling a Ross–Monmouth train. Note the camping coach at the disused platform. *Below*: Tintern station, on the Chepstow–Monmouth branch, restored to its original condition, and in use as a picnic centre. (*R.O. Tuck, J.H.R. Page*)

the far side of the valley was the only solution, but the viaduct was forever a visible reminder of its presence.

## The Midland route to Swansea

Today, perhaps, it is a little surprising to realise that the line from Hereford to Swansea via Brecon was worked by the Midland Railway and its successor, the LMS. This was the situation before 1932, when following the traffic pooling agreement with the GWR, the LMS finally withdrew from the Ynisygeinon to Brecon stretch which the GWR had taken over ten years before when it absorbed the N&B at the Grouping. Nationalisation transferred the whole line from Hereford to Ynisygeinon Junction, and the LMS line south of there (described in Chapter 9), to the Western Region. Even so, the ghosts of the Midland and LMS were never far away. Their spirit haunted the line right to the end, for the last regular passenger train from Brecon on 29 January 1962, the 9.35pm to Builth Wells was hauled by an LMS Class 2MT 2–6–0.

The Midland entered the area following the failure of the GWR to assist the ailing HH&B, and was one of those myopic incidents that recur throughout the history of the GWR, and frequently to the benefit of the Midland Railway. By 1869 the HH&B's chickens had come home to roost. Its earlier machinations lost it the southern section of its projected route beyond Three Cocks Junction to its rivals the MWR and the B&M, and ultimately left it in the hands of Savin, the contractor and operator of the two other companies. Mismanagement by the B&M with which it was briefly amalgamated (until the union was declared illegal) left it in a hopeless position. It therefore welcomed the offer of the Midland Railway to work its traffic from 1869, which was the prelude to amalgamation in 1874 and total absorption in 1876.

The N&B was not so lucky. A badly-managed colliery railway, it over-reached itself by extending to Brecon from the original terminus of its line from Neath (Riverside) at Onllwyn. Glad of the support of the Midland, it never ceased to complain about the proportion of the receipts it received for granting running powers over the bulk of its system. 1889 saw the N&B sufficiently outraged at the treatment meted out to it that it ordered the withdrawal of the Midland from its system. This laughable display of independence lasted three weeks. After this time the Midland returned, and the humiliated N&B continued to receive the same proportion of the gross receipts of the Brecon section of its line as before—30 per cent.

Having succeeded in its objective of reaching Swansea, and having done so with the minimum capital outlay, it is surprising that the Midland never fully developed the potential of this through route. It could have become the Settle & Carlisle line of South Wales. After all, was it not competing with its greatest rival, the LNWR, and was not the position of Swansea as a terminal point of that system analogous to Carlisle? Similarly the Black Mountain and the uplands of Fforest Fawr (remarkably treeless despite its name—large forest), have a grandeur the equal of Pen-y-Ghent and Blea Moor. But no through express services were ever run by the Midland or the LMS. Not for this line Class 2P 4–4–0s or Compounds with lake-coloured rakes of Bain corridor coaches, later followed by Baby Scots or Jubilees with maroon stock in tow. The only through workings were to and from Birmingham by carriages attached to certain trains. Despite the lack of fast trains the motive power of the line was not without interest, for in 1874 the Midland drafted in 0–4–4Ts for the passenger services. They ran daily from Hereford through to Swansea and return. This locomotive type continued to work these services until the LMS withdrew from the Ynisygeinon to Brecon section in 1932. For 58 years these diminutive stalwarts plied back and forth over the mountains, their daily journeys of $79\frac{1}{4}$ miles each way ranking as one of the longest tank engine workings in the country.

The journey from Hereford traversed a route of contrasts, a reflection of earlier times which persists in the relics that remain, some 23 years after the last section closed. Physical remains are few, but the scant number are of considerable interest. At Hereford the first few hundred yards of the line to Brecon have not only survived, but are steam-operated. This short section is used as a running line and access to BR proper by *King George*

*V*, and the other locomotives at the Bulmer Railway Centre. In retirement, as one might say, it now carries locomotives far heavier than were ever allowed in years gone by.

Nothing remains of Kinnersley station (SO 342488), but look closely at the adjacent road bridge. The short length of wooden fencing, with diagonal instead of vertical boards, still reminds one of its Midland origins, as does the maker's plate on the bridge parapet, proudly proclaiming its manufacturer, 'W. RICHARDS & SON, LEICESTER—1901'. Further west, Midland Railway reminders can be found at Eardisley (SO 313485) and Hay-on-Wye (SO 231428). Both station sites are now privately-owned, but in what were their goods yards the solid red brick goods sheds remain in daily use. At Three Cocks Junction (SO 167377) there is a sudden change, for now one is on what was the Cambrian Railways section. The solidly-constructed stone station building still clearly proclaims its origins, for it has been little altered over the years since closure. The station site is now the area's Calor gas distribution depot, the station building being the depot's office. Of the B&M there is nothing, and only Craig-y-Nos station remains on the N&B section, standing on the high moorland above the Swansea valley at SN 854158. Until a few years ago a large notice was attached to the north wall of the station building detailing the history of the station. It did not however record the date on which steam briefly returned to the area. This was in the summer of 1971 when the section near Craig-y-Nos was used for the filming of *Young Winston*, the story of the early career of Sir Winston Churchill. For the purposes of the film these South Wales uplands became the South African veldt, where the disguised Great Western Society's Collett 0-4-2T 1466 (complete with 'armour plate') was ambushed by the Boers.

The contrasts in the few physical remains accurately reflected the changing character of the line as one travelled westward from Hereford. The rich farming areas of the Wye valley, where the rail traveller once passed beneath the nonchalant gaze of red Hereford cattle, were charming and tranquil. Gradually as one climbed out of the Wye valley when crossing the watershed to the Usk the scenery changed as the wooded hills pressed closer, and bare mountains were viewed in the distance for the first time. Finally, behind dimunitive motive power, one climbed into these bare mountains searching for the windswept pass between their dominating heights. Here with trees and hedge-rows left far behind, the only observers of the travellers' passage were sheep, the only animals the thin grass could support.

# CHAPTER 3

# Monmouth

## WHAT MIGHT HAVE BEEN

That not one section of any of the branches that converged upon Monmouth was not preserved is a tragedy. The Wye, which encompassed the two separate branch lines from Chepstow to Monmouth, and thence to Ross-on-Wye, rightfully claims to be the most beautiful river in Britain. This was recognised in 1971 when 125 square miles of the Wye valley from Chepstow to north of Ross-on-Wye was designated an area of 'Outstanding Natural Beauty'. While this beauty is open to the walker, only congested roads provide a route for the majority of tourists. That the beauties of the Wye cannot be savoured at leisure from the comfort of a railway carriage is a great loss. The third branch from Monmouth to Pontypool Road, via Usk and Little Mill Junction was hardly less beautiful, though there is none of the grandeur of the Wye in the rolling hills that guard the valleys of the Trothy and the Olway. To think of the preservation of these branches is to think of what might have been, and 'what-might-have-been' is the story of Monmouth and its railways.

Had all the schemes in which Monmouth was involved in the mid-19th century come to fruition the town would have been on through routes to South Wales, London, Liverpool, and most interestingly Northampton. Closer to home Bristol, Gloucester, Worcester and Hereford figured prominently in destinations of proposed railways. In the event none of these schemes was completed, and those that were, were more modest.

Monmouth's first railway came from the west, but its destination was actually Coleford, in the Forest of Dean. Its purpose was to carry iron ore principally to furnaces near Nantyglo, together with pitwood, and also farm produce for the increasing population of the industrial areas. The Coleford, Monmouth, Usk & Pontypool Railway was incorporated on 20 August 1853 as a

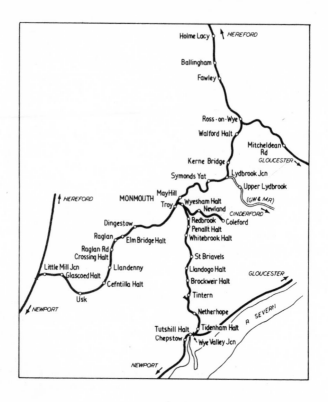

single-line railway from the Newport, Abergavenny & Hereford
Railway at Little Mill Junction to Wyesham (across the Wye
from Monmouth). By use of the Monmouth tramroad (a horse-
worked line dating from 1810) it was to gain access to Coleford.
Completed to Monmouth (Troy) on 12 October 1857 the extension to Wyesham (on what later became the Chepstow branch)
was not opened until 1 July 1861. The extension to Coleford
was ultimately built by the Coleford Railway; its story is outside the scope of this book.

Still anxious to obtain the status of a town through which a
railway would pass, and not (effectively) terminate, Monmouth
interests were active in the promotion of the Ross & Monmouth
Railway. This proposed a line between these two towns along
the Wye valley, and connecting with the Hereford, Ross &
Gloucester Railway which opened in 1855. Eighteen frustrating
years were to pass before this single line was completed on 4
August 1873. This line was thought of in its early years, when

railway promotion was still a force in the land, as a vital link to the north. Chepstow, at the mouth of the Wye, had no direct northerly outlet, being on the South Wales to Gloucester line. It was a desire for such a connection, coupled with the prospect of improved transport for the industries along the Wye, that brought into being the Wye Valley Railway. Like the Ross & Monmouth many years passed between inception and completion. Not until 1 November 1876 did the first train run through to Monmouth from Wye Valley Junction on the main line ¾-mile east of Chepstow, using the Wyesham extension of the erstwhile CMU&PR for its access to Troy station.

The railways to Monmouth were now complete, and the town had its desired connections. Alas, they came too late. The frenzied construction of railways that characterised the mid-19th century was over, and industrial traffic patterns had altered significantly. Forest of Dean ore had been quickly superseded by Northamptonshire or imported ores in the hungry furnaces to the west. The former was now carried by railways better placed for direct transport to South Wales since the demise of the proposed extension of the Northampton & Banbury Railway to Ross-on-Wye. The GWR absorbed the CMU&PR (as part of the West Midland Railway) in 1863; the Ross and Wye Valley companies were effectively GWR satellites, and worked by it from their completion. The GWR needed no alternative routes to those it already had, so these lines never developed beyond rural branch lines. They slid quietly into an unhurried existence in picturesque surroundings with a pattern of working that changed little with the passing years. Passenger services to Chepstow and Ross ceased on 5 January 1959, the service to Pontypool Road having been withdrawn on 30 May 1955. Freight working continued over some sections until 1964/5. Only two short sections remain : from Little Mill Junction to Glascoed, and Wye Valley Junction to Tidenham quarry, both worked as sidings.

### The Pontypool Branch

Diverging at Little Mill Junction, two miles north east of Pontypool Road, the branch ran down the valley of the

Berthin Brook to Usk, and beyond swung up the Olway Brook, crossed the watershed near Raglan to the Trothy, down whose vale it ran to Monmouth. Hemmed in by closely crowding low hills west of Usk, the landscape became more open and rolling as that town was left behind. From Usk to Monmouth one can still savour the scenic delights of this little line for the main A449/A40 road follows its trackbed with few deviations.

Each of the branch's stations was a delight, and that at Raglan can still be seen alongside the A40, its principal building of red brick remaining intact as a store for the Highways Department of the Gwent County Council. Apart from Troy station only Usk had two platforms. This station stood immediately west of Usk tunnel. Carved through sandstone, its rock has provided fossil exhibits now in the National Museum at Cardiff. The station was so cramped that the goods yard was $\frac{1}{4}$-mile away across the river, which was spanned by a plate-girder viaduct on sandstone piers.

For years, apart from the occasional excursion, little was done to stimulate passenger traffic. However some attempts were made in the 1930s with the addition of an evening train from Monmouth, and the opening of a halt at Elm Bridge. This was not the last halt built, however. At the eleventh hour Cefntilla Halt was opened on 14 June 1954. Less than 16ft in length, with no ramps, its only facilities were a nameboard, a safety rail, and a solitary lamp. It closed after the passing of the last passenger train on 30 May 1955.

### The Chepstow and Ross Branches

Crossing and recrossing the Welsh border until north of Monmouth, these two branches ran alongside the most beautiful river in Britain. Even before the Wye valley proper was reached the view from the top of the climb from Wye Valley Junction, of the broad estuary of the Severn, was outstanding. The descent through the narrow bore of Tidenham tunnel was a dark prelude to the beauties that lay beyond its northern end, all the more breathtaking for their sudden appearance.

Tintern station lay beyond the ruins of the world-renowned 12th century Cistercian Abbey, and the long-forgotten branch to Tintern Wire Works. The final approach was through a short tunnel beyond which one was immediately precipitated across the river on a lattice girder bridge, and on to a curving embankment to the station. Through the combined efforts of the Gwent County Council, the Countryside Commission and the Monmouth District Council, Tintern station is still with us. Both station and signalbox have been faithfully rebuilt as the centrepiece of a picnic site and exhibition centre. The site has been grassed-over and the trackbed, from the river bridge to the Brockweir road has been converted into a footpath. This path is the first of three sections of trackbed between Chepstow and Symonds Yat that have been dedicated as part of the Wye Valley walk. The little museum contains a well-illustrated history of the branch. The authorities concerned are to be congratulated for their endeavours; would that others had been so enlightened.

Near Monmouth the valley broadens and the branch descended in a majestic sweep from Wyesham, crossed the river on a lattice span and strode across the water meadows on a sandstone viaduct of 20 arches to Troy station.

Whether the beauty of the Ross branch through the twisting valley east of Monmouth equalled or surpassed that of the wider sweeps to the south is a matter of taste. Each is superb in its own way. Surprisingly, the branch was once favoured by royalty. In the early years of this century Symonds Yat was visited by King Edward VII. Once a passing place, the station had a neat single-storey wooden building devoid of any awning. So narrow was the station site that the signalbox situated on the riverside platform was actually over the river, being supported by stout steel struts. None of this now remains, the station site is a car park for the Royal Hotel that Edward VII once visited, but the attractive approach from the south can still be walked. About $1\frac{1}{4}$ miles of trackbed forms the last section of the Wye Valley walk.

## Monmouth

Monmouth (Troy) was the focus of all the branches from east, west and south. Yet in the tradition of the country station it was not even in Monmouth, but stood beneath a hill nearly a mile to the south-west of the town. Facilities included a single-storey ticket office, waiting room, porters' room etc, with a full-length awning; a small shelter with a similar awning stood on the opposite platform. A covered footbridge linked the two. Immediately west, on the branch to Usk, was a short tunnel (148yds) of twin bore. Only the northernmost line was a running line, the other was a siding. Goods facilities were adequately provided for in a yard containing six sidings, on one of which stood the large goods shed, and on another, cattle pens. The separation of the branches to Ross and Chepstow occurred as a double junction at the east end of the platforms. Movements were controlled by the adjacent signalbox, which like all major buildings was built of the attractive local sandstone. The station building stands today, altered and extended for use by a local haulage contractor; the goods shed and yard are used by an agricultural merchant and a coal merchant respectively.

From at least the turn of the century until World War II the services on the branches from Pontypool Road to Monmouth and Monmouth to Ross-on-Wye were run as a through service. Initially four through trains daily were run, but later this was cut to three. These were in addition to shorter workings, *viz*. Pontypool Road to Usk or Monmouth, or Ross-on-Wye to Lydbrook Junction. The Chepstow branch services were always separate, and for many years consisted of five trains each way daily, and until 1916 augmented by a connecting service off the Coleford branch. Connections between all these services were made three times a day, giving Troy its busiest periods. The first connection was about 9.00am, followed by two others at around midday and 4.00pm, the precise times varying slightly over the years.

For many years the goods yard was kept busy by three workings daily, one each from each of the branches. The first, from Chepstow, arrived at 10.45am and departed at 12.20pm. The Pontypool Road freight arrived 25 minutes after the Chepstow train and hung around until 5.00pm. Finally the Ross-on-Wye working rattled in at 1.40pm, departing an hour and five minutes later. At midday Troy station really bustled with three passenger and two freight trains busying themselves within its precincts.

Motive power over the years was provided by six-coupled saddle and pannier tanks, 517 and 14xx (or should I say 48xx) 0–4–2Ts, and in the 1950s the occasional GWR-designed diesel railcar. With the exception of 45xx 2–6–2Ts nothing larger was allowed on any of the branches. In turn, these classes busied themselves in this delightful backwater for over a century. Now, where the shrill whistle of the steam locomotive was once heard, the air throbs with the sound of the diesel-engined road juggernaut.

# CHAPTER 4

# Pontypool and Abergavenny

## GATEWAY TO THE WEST

To drive railways westward from Pontypool and Abergavenny one had to have a great financial prize, and a singleness of purpose bordering on the fanatic. In the mid-19th century the prize existed; the wealth generated by the ironworks of Merthyr and Dowlais, with connections to the lesser works strung along the northern borders of Glamorganshire and Monmouthshire as bonuses, together with the rapidly-developing coal trade. The Merthyr district supported four great works, of which Dowlais was recognised as the largest in the world at that time. To understand why singleness of purpose was needed, a glance at the geography of South Wales will quickly make this clear. To reach the Taff valley from the east, three steep-sided river valleys had to be crossed to make use of the only convenient western exit from Pontypool. To reach Merthyr from Abergavenny an ascent to the uplands at about 1200ft, across the heads of these same valleys, was necessary, a convenient westward entrance being provided by the Clydach gorge. By either route the civil engineering was difficult and expensive.

The westward route from Pontypool, built by the Newport, Abergavenny & Hereford Railway was completed to a junction with the Taff Vale Railway at Quakers Yard in 1858, and ultimately formed a through route to Swansea. This was opened in 1864 when the extension was completed to the Vale of Neath Railway at Middle Duffryn in the Aberdare valley. This latter was a broad gauge line, over which the third rail was laid in the same year. Both companies were absorbed by the GWR, and from 1864 to 1922 this through route was that company's busiest freight line across South Wales.

It fell to the LNWR between 1862 and 1879 to build the

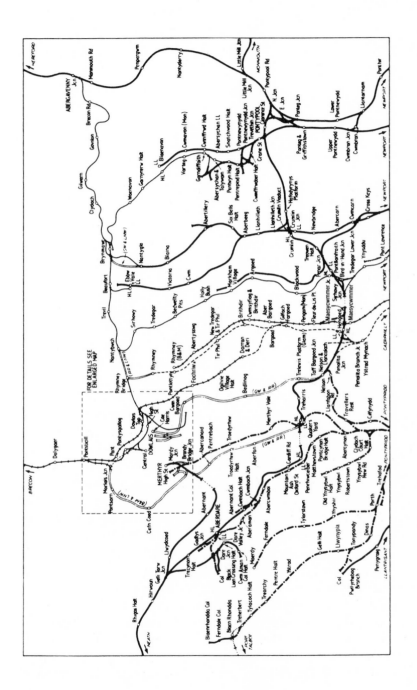

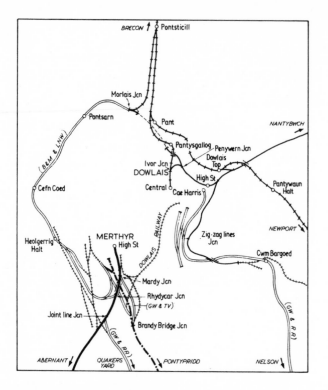

'heads of the valleys' route, parts of which it built or worked
in conjunction with local companies. Ultimately Merthyr and
Dowlais were served by six railways, and to fully understand the
development of the lines built westward from Pontypool and
Abergavenny it is first necessary to briefly describe the growth of
railways to Merthyr and Dowlais.

The first arrival, opened on 12 April 1841, was the Taff Vale
Railway. It entered Merthyr from the south to its original
terminus at Plymouth Street. The second, from the east, was the
Dowlais Railway, opened on 21 August 1851 to connect the ironworks to the Taff Vale system. Then from the west came the
broad gauge Vale of Neath Railway, completed to its High
Street terminus in 1853. It was altered to mixed gauge in 1864.
The Brecon & Merthyr Railway entered in 1868 from the north,
sweeping in an immense curve to join the V of N line (by now
GWR-owned) at Rhydycar Junction. From here running
powers allowed it into High Street. The B&M line was reached
by the LNWR from 1 June 1879, whence that company's

traffic also entered Merthyr. TVR passenger traffic was diverted into High Street from 1 August 1877. Railway development was completed in 1886 with the arrival from the south of the Quaker's Yard & Merthyr Joint line. Promoted by the Rhymney and Great Western Railways it ran up the west bank of the Taff to Joint Line Junction, to join the ex-V of N line.

Apart from the Dowlais Railway, connections to this town were made in 1863 and 1873 respectively by the B&M and LNWR. In 1876 the Taff Bargoed branch (again RR&GWR joint) opened from Llancaiach on the Pontypool to Neath line. It formed the Dowlais works' only direct connection to Cardiff for its exports. More importantly, it provided access for imported iron ore, since local sources were by now exhausted. Only the single line of this connection remained at the end of the Dowlais railways, before the closure of the last remaining portion of the ironworks in 1987. Today Merthyr itself is only served by the singled TVR route.

As elsewhere, tramway development preceded the introduction of the rail system. Unlike similar developments to the east, around such towns as Tredegar, Ebbw Vale and Blaenavon, only one tramway in the Merthyr area developed beyond the stage of a feeder from quarry, mine or canal. This was the Penydarren tramway, opened in 1803. It ran from Penydarren to a place known as the 'basin' near Abercynon, with extensions to Dowlais and the Morlais quarries. Never fully converted to a railway, it fell into disuse south of Merthyr in the middle 1880s, although a converted section within Merthyr remained in use for a further 40 years or so. Its course is still visible near its southern end only, where it parallels the TVR line for a short distance. Strictly speaking this tramroad is outside the scope of this book, but no mention of railway development in the Merthyr area can omit referring to this historic tramway on which the first steam locomotive ran on 21 February 1804.

## Westward from Pontypool

The Newport, Abergavenny & Hereford Railway's westward drive from Pontypool was never envisaged as a through route across the South Wales valleys. That it became one in 1864 under the GWR, and not merely a branch to the TVR as originally intended, was a chance of timing. It neared the entrance of the Cynon valley shortly after the start of the coal mining expansion that supplied a traffic to succeed that of iron, and maintain the viability of the local rail system for the next century, and was ideally placed for shipment to English outlets, for the export trade was still in its infancy.

The first section of this through route to be opened was in fact the western end, in the shape of the broad gauge Vale of Neath Railway incorporated in 1846. It was intended to build from Neath to Merthyr, with a branch to Aberdare. In the event the Aberdare branch opened first in September 1851. Later extension by this company and the Aberdare Valley Railway extended the broad gauge to Middle Duffryn, near Mountain Ash, by the end of 1857. Merthyr was reached in November 1853, and a branch to the Dare and Aman valleys was commenced in 1852. The V of N did not prosper as it should have done, principally due to its gauge. Matters would have probably rested there, and the company languished as a local colliery line had it not been for a proposal from the West Midland Railway, as successor to the NA&H. A proposal made with the express intention of providing a standard gauge through route from Pontypool to Swansea.

The Pontypool connection commenced in 1847 with the incorporation of the Newport, Abergavenny and Hereford (Taff Vale Extension) Railway, a standard gauge line to be built westward from Pontypool and making a connection with the TVR at Quakers Yard, which was completed in 1858. Before completion however, it obtained sanction to extend to join the V of N at Middle Duffryn. Shortly afterwards, as the West Midland Railway, of which it had become a part in 1860, it proposed the laying of the third rail over that system. Connection was completed in August 1864, by which time the West Midland had become absorbed by the GWR. February 1865 saw the V of N enter the fold, thus providing the GWR with a standard gauge route across South Wales' richest valleys.

Through passenger services began immediately, at the modest

*Plates 5 and 6.* Local trains. *Above*: Ex-GWR 0-4-2T No 1455 at Monmouth (Troy) station on 3 January 1959, the last day of ordinary passenger services. *Below*: Ex-GWR 0-6-0PT No 9644 at Pontllanfraith on the former LNWR Sirhowy Valley line with a train from Tredegar to Risca. (*R.O. Tuck, R.E. Toop*)

Plates 7 and 8. Pontypool–Neath. *Above:* Crumlin viaduct in the last days of steam. An unidentified GW 2-6-2T heads west across the unique structure 200ft above the valley floor. *Below:* In later years LMS8F locomotives worked some services. No 48761 is near Mountain Ash on 1 July 1963. (*Hamwell Jones Collection, D. K. Jones*)

rate of two up and three down trains daily. By 1910 this had increased to six up and five down, although running times were little altered from some 50 years before. Stock was vastly improved with Dean bogie coaches much in evidence, handled by sturdy 0–6–0STs. New and powerful standard tank locomotives had by the 1930s brought through times down to around $1\frac{3}{4}$ hours, despite a rise from 15 to 23 stops. Post-war services never rose to these levels or timings, and as the daylight faded on 13 June 1964, 2–6–2T 4121 crossed Crumlin viaduct with the last westbound passenger train. At 11.10pm the last eastbound train steamed quietly into Pontypool Road station. The line was officially closed as a through route two days later, $3\frac{1}{2}$ months short of its centenary.

From a freight standpoint the line was one of the busiest on the GWR system. Churchward designed locomotives specially for it, the outside-framed 2–6–0 Aberdare class, although his later 4200 class 2–8–0T, and its later 2–8–2T variant the 7200 class, were regular locomotives for many years. The lifeblood of the line flowed from the colliery connections it made, either in the valleys through which it ran or from the branches and junctions that connected it to the local railways in the valleys it crossed. In all, eight major junctions and five branches made connections, two of the latter remaining open today worked as sidings from the remnants of the remaining local railways.

Of the countless thousands of coal trains that ran along this line one deserves special mention. At 9.50am on 9 January 1886 it left Aberdare hauling 14 laden coal wagons and two brake vans, and headed for Salisbury. It was in fact the first train to run through the Severn Tunnel, being essentially a trial run some nine months before the official opening. As a matter of interest it did not run via Pontypool, but was routed over the LNWR Sirhowy branch at Pontllanfraith. This was a frequently adopted course to avoid congestion at Pontypool.

The line's busiest period, its 'finest hour', was during World War I. For the duration of that war the Home Fleet, based at Scapa Flow, was dependent upon a continuous supply of Welsh steam coal. Over 11,500 special coal trains were routed via Pontypool Road, most of which came from the Neath line, destined for Grangemouth, Glasgow or perhaps Tyneside. One should also not forget the inevitable returning empties, either. By the time of World War II it was not necessary to repeat such feats. However, the strategic potential of the line was still recognised, together with its vulnerable points, a recognition that stretched to Germany. In 1940 the Luftwaffe was issued with a series of books containing photographs, taken by agents before hostilities began, of strategic targets in Great Britain. Amongst these photographs was one of Crumlin viaduct, complete with a 5700 class 0–6–0PT.

Above all else it was the line's switchback gradients and civil engineering features that command attention. Between Pontypool and Neath it ran along four river valleys, crossed three watersheds, and spanned a further four rivers. To do this required four tunnels, and three viaducts, including the graceful Hengoed and the unique Crumlin. Throughout the line massive embankments and steep gradients were the order of the day.

Nowhere is the engineering ingenuity of those who built this line better illustrated than in the design and construction of the Crumlin viaduct. At Crumlin the Ebbw valley is narrow and precipitous. This combination ensures that under certain conditions wind speeds can become abnormally high. This fact dictated that a rigid stone viaduct could not be economically built with sufficient strength to withstand the expected buffeting. The design of braced cast-iron tubes and girders was accepted, since it reduced to a minimum the cross section exposed to the wind, and the forces on the structure. The result was an engineering masterpiece, both practical and graceful. It was actually built as two spans (separated by an intermediate hill), one of 1066ft and the other of 584ft; the maximum height was 200ft. Scheduled for preservation, but receiving no maintenance after closure, its ageing fabric deteriorated rapidly, and it was dismantled in 1967. Only the abutments high up on the valley sides mark its position. Prior to dismantling, it became internationally famous for a totally different reason, following its use in a chase sequence for the film *Arabesque*, featuring Sophia Loren and Gregory Peck.

## Branches off the Pontypool to Neath line

Whilst the Pontypool to Neath line was best known as a cross-valleys link, it must not be forgotten that the original intention of both its constituents was to reach Merthyr. Two branches achieved this aim. The first was off the V of N section from Gelli Tarw Junction, between Hirwaun and Aberdare. Construction of its principal civil engineering features, the Merthyr tunnel, and the heavy earthworks in the Taff valley, delayed the opening until 2 November 1853. In all it took six years to build, and bankrupted two contractors. Despite its lowly status in the eyes of Brunel, he still contrived to stamp his personality on the line. Merthyr station was a typical broad gauge terminus, and until the 1950s retained its distinctive all-over roof. Only two intermediate stations were built. One of these was at Abernant, a district of the Cynon valley noted for its ironworks. Here Brunel was at his most fanciful. Until rebuilt, the single-storey waiting room and ticket office sported tall chimneys decorated in the Italian style, complete with campaniles, very like those on Chippenham station when originally built.

The second branch to reach Merthyr, built jointly by the Great Western and Rhymney Railways, deviated northwards from a little to the west of Quakers Yard (HL) and ran up the western side of the Taff valley. It joined the ex-V of N branch at the prosaically named Joint Line Junction, about $1\frac{1}{4}$ miles from High Street Station. Built with a ruling gradient of 1 in 51 and completed in 1886, it at last gave the GWR independent and relatively easy access to Merthyr. The great iron metropolis was by then past the peak of its greatness, and the line never flourished as was hoped. Its most striking feature was the stone viaduct by which it crossed the Taff at Quakers Yard, adjacent to a similar structure that carried the Neath line. Mining subsidence undermined both viaducts, and for many years they remained in use with the arches shored up with heavy timbers, and subject to a 10mph speed restriction. When viewed whilst travelling by train from Cardiff to Merthyr they looked quite alarming.

Brunel's personality was indelibly stamped on a further branch from the V of N system, which ran from Gelli Tarw Junction southeast to Cwmaman, with an offshoot to Cwmdare. Although only a mineral line, off what he considered a mere branch to the South Wales Railway, he graced it with two of his famous fan trestle viaducts, the Dare and the Gamlyn. Both survived unaltered for about 90 years, until well after the closure of the branch. They were not dismantled until 1947, having outlived their more famous Cornish counterparts by about 15 years.

Built piecemeal between 1854 and 1857, the line followed colliery development in the two valleys from Gelli Tàrw Junction to Cwmaman, and from Dare Junction to Nantymelin Colliery. It was joined by the Dare Valley Railway (later a branch of the Taff Vale Railway) in 1866. This ran from Dare Valley Junction, on the TVR at Aberdare, to Bwllfa Dare Colliery. These mineral lines went quietly about their business for many years. The most noteworthy event was the introduction of a motor train service in 1906, which lasted until September 1924. But for the events of 1932–1935, this little network would by now have disappeared from memory, for all except the short TVR section, closed in 1939. At that time, in the depths of the great depression, thoughts turned to the welfare of the local children. Six churches in Cwmaman, and two in nearby Godreaman, arranged Sunday School outings in these years, travelling alternately to Porthcawl and Barry Island. A simple enough event one might think, but not for the GWR. It baulked at sending excursion trains on to the line, preferring to start from Aberdare (HL) and merely providing a train from Cwmaman to Black Lion Halt, about ½-mile from the High Level station. They suggested that the children walk the intervening distance. The churches would have nothing of this high-handed attitude, not the least of their arguments being the notorious fickleness of the Welsh weather. Eventually the GWR relented, and at 7.20am on 23 July 1932 the first of two fully-laden excursion trains departed from Cwmaman for Porthcawl. Over 1700 children and adults travelled that day, for the rather exorbitant (for 1932) fares of 1s 9d (9p) for children and 3s 6d (17½p) for adults. Rolling stock on these trips consisted of 6-wheel coaches usually headed by open-cab pannier tanks from the local shed, the latter too on a rare excursion from the area. The GWR never quibbled over arrangements in future years and although short-lived, these annual trips off the Cwmaman branch remain as vivid childhood memories amongst the older generation of the area.

## North of Pontypool

Although the fame of Pontypool as a railway junction rested on its countrywide connections via the GWR, a line of the old Monmouthshire Railway to Blaenavon also passed through the town. Originally a tramroad, running from the canal head at Pontynewynydd, dating from 1796, it ran along the valley floor to Blaenavon Ironworks. It was rebuilt by the Monmouthshire Company as a northern extension of their Newport & Pontypool Railway in 1854. Typical of its breed, it served the area well, passing away almost unnoticed in the holocaust of closures in 1962.

It is best remembered, not so much for itself, but for two branches that made connection to it. The valley of the Aponlwyd and its tributaries are narrow and steep-sided, even by South Wales standards. As a result, gradients on connecting lines from local collieries were exceptionally steep. These collieries were mainly to the west of the Pontypool–Blaenavon line, and from 1879 were much better served by a high-level line built by the Great Western from Trevethin Junction to Abersychan and Talywain to join the branch from Brynmawr built by the LNWR. The section to Abersychan and Talywain closed in 1980 and is described in the Postscript; the northern section will be referred to later.

Two small branches, however, to the Cwmffrwdoer and Cwmnantddu valleys, remained connected to the lower line. At Pontnewynydd junction a branch veered sharply west for about ½-mile to Branches Fork Junction, where the lines to these two valleys diverged. Although short, they were exceptionally steep. Gradients on the Cwmffrwdoer branch were 1 in 22, and on the Cwmnantddu even steeper at 1 in 19. Their methods of working were naturally exceptional. Locomotives had always to propel empty trains up the inclines, and be coupled in front of loaded trains coming down. Further it was required that two guards be carried, one of whom rode in the leading wagon, and the other in the guard's van, which had to be coupled next to the loco-motive. This latter requirement restricted the driver's view of the train, and any signals given by the guard in the leading wagon. As a result between 1888 and 1890 the GWR built four special brake vans for these duties. They had roofless verandahs at each end, unlike the usual GWR design, and the central cabin which had a steeply-pitched roof was limited in height to 6ft giving an overall height of only 9ft 10½in from rail level. Known as the 'Noah's Arks' they served the line, to which they were restricted, for about 60 years, being replaced by two of similar design in 1949. The last survivor was unceremoniously burnt at a Newport scrapyard on 24 October 1968.

## The Dowlais Railway

Rising from the Cardiff road at SO 055054 is a straight wide swathe of grass running between the houses, until it becomes lost in the jumble of overgrown tips clustered around the derelict Dowlais Iron Works. This green swathe is not an accident of nature or an attempt by the local authority to brighten one of the most desolated towns of South Wales. It is the course of the Dowlais Railway. The line, 1 miles 68 chains long was opened on 21 August 1851, the lower 70 chains being a 1 in 12 double tracked rope-worked incline, powered by a stationary engine. It was built by the Dowlais Iron Company, and ran to a passenger station alongside the Merthyr–Abergavenny road; beyond, an extension led through the works to quarries. Today only the site of the incline is recognisable, although the once uniform gradient has now been terraced.

Built for the Dowlais Company's traffic, the line also operated a passenger and public goods service in its early years in connec-tion with the Taff Vale Railway. The former commenced in 1851, and until discontinued in 1854 following an accident, was well patronised. The public goods service lasted longer, ceasing in 1876. The line continued in use well into this century, operations finally ceasing in October 1930.

The operation of the incline was extremely dangerous. For example in the Taff Vale Railway rule book for 1853, rule 1992 states:

The Bankrider of the rope nearest Merthyr is always to ride (sitting) upon the inside buffer, and the Bankrider of the other rope is always to ride (sitting) upon the buffer next up the hill; and in the event of either having occasion to jump off or leave his seat he must be particularly careful that he does not come in contact with the opposite, or his own run, or the slope or with either of the ropes, or injure himself, by falling slipping or otherwise.

In the light of present day industrial safety legislation one can only be amazed that such a rule could ever have existed.

### The North Western line to Merthyr

Even though built piecemeal by four companies, the railway from Abergavenny to Merthyr was conceived as a through route. Its origins date from 1859 when the Merthyr, Tredegar & Abergavenny Railway was empowered to build its line via the Clydach gorge, and to purchase and convert an old tramway, known as Bailey's tramroad. Having reached Abergavenny in 1854, the LNWR's first attempt to reach Merthyr was by running powers over the NA&H Taff Vale extension, and the TVR from 1858. This was not to the liking of the LNWR. The answer to their problem came with the MT&A's direct thrust into the hills west of Abergavenny. Friendly approaches, together with assistance during construction resulted in an agreement to lease the line in 1862. This was followed by absorption by the LNWR four years later. So it was that when the MT&A opened from Abergavenny to Brynmawr in 1862 it was worked by the North Western. In 1864 it was extended to Nantybwch, where it was joined by the Sirhowy Railway four years later.

Following the opening of branches to Blaenavon and Ebbw Vale, the next extension westward was made jointly with the Rhymney Railway and opened in 1871. Running to the town of Rhymney itself, it deviated from the direct route to Merthyr.

This was a shrewd move by the LNWR as it gave it access to
Cardiff, as described in Chapter 6. Dowlais was reached in
1873 by an extension of this joint line at Rhymney Bridge,
despite a defiant rearguard action by the B&M to prevent this
interloper invading its territory. Eleven years had now passed
since the LNWR had set off for Merthyr, and another six lay
ahead before it reached there in 1879 by building a line behind
and beneath Dowlais to reach the Merthyr branch of the B&M.
It had been prepared to build its own line the whole way, an
intention that so frightened the B&M that it agreed not only
to the use of its branch by the North Western, but also to its
ownership becoming joint with that company.

The railway from Abergavenny to Merthyr was the most
spectacular in South Wales. The climb up the Clydach gorge,
a 7-mile ascent, much at 1 in 34/37/38, with the upper portion
cut into a hillside shelf, was breathtaking. Beyond Brynmawr,
and rarely descending below 1200ft, the line undulated across
the despoiled moorland and the heads of the mining valleys to
Dowlais. Even in the height of summer this treeless waste is
bleak, in winter it is forbidding and dangerous. Dowlais (High
Street) marked the start of the steep descent to Morlais Junction
and then over the B&M/LNWR joint section to Merthyr which
was described in Chapter 2. This descent of about 6½ miles
mainly between 1 in 40/50 was not without its surprises. The
start was through the town and behind the famous ironworks,
before Morlais tunnel was entered. Beyond came the surprise
as one emerged into the wooded valley of the Taf Fechan, but
beyond Pontsarn the scene changed once more as one continued
the descent to Merthyr.

Closed to through passenger traffic in January 1958, isolated
portions remained open until 1963. A great deal has disappeared
since then, notably beneath the A465 'Heads of the Valleys'
road, but the route up the Clydach gorge can still be clearly
traced. This will probably remain for generations as a monument to Victorian enterprise, tenacity and skill. With the exception of the two viaducts on the B&M/LNWR joint section,
dealt with in Chapter 2, only the noble 9-arch viaduct that
can be seen to the north of the A465 at SO 133109 remains of

the many similar structures large and small that once helped to carry this line across this inhospitable terrain. But whereas bridges and viaducts have been felled the three tunnels remain. Those at Clydach and Gelli Felen are high up in the Clydach gorge. Both are of twin bore with massive brick retaining walls alongside their inner bores, which were opened up when the line was doubled in 1877. They were constructed where the curves of the old tramroad were too sharp for its railway successor. The third tunnel is at Dowlais and the south portal still bears the proud legend 'JOHN GARDNER ENGINEER, JOHN MACRAY CONTRACTOR, 1879'.

Along the lower part of the route the station buildings, of which only Govilon remains, were of stone and complemented their surroundings. So too did the graceful bridge with its six pairs of slender columns, delicately cross-braced, that spanned the Usk just outside Abergavenny. From Brynmawr to Dowlais it was a different story. As with most lines built through industrial areas, the minimum was spent in the way of embellishment or decoration. Paradoxically, a flimsy construction could not be tolerated with structures built at about 1200ft and in positions that afforded little or no shelter from winter storms. With the exception of Beaufort the stations on this section were of wooden construction, as for that matter were the platforms themselves at Brynmawr and Dowlais (High Street). Distinctive features were the footbridges which in LNWR days were enclosed against the elements, with that at Nantybwch not even having glass-panelled sides as at Brynmawr and Rhymney Bridge. The only station sheltered in any major way was Beaufort, which was in a cutting. However, the protection this afforded was illusory, for in the winter of 1947 a train was stranded here and completely disappeared from view for several weeks.

It was not a line for the faint hearted or over-imaginative. Pitch-black windswept nights, often of bitter cold, in which anything loose on these lonely stations would rattle and creak, could on occasions make even the most strong-willed jump. So for that matter could the dark shape of a wandering sheep or pony looming out of the darkness into the isolated pool of a station light.

Five valleys were served by branches, of which the longest ran down the Sirhowy and is described in Chapter 5. Of the remaining, two were quite short, only about 1½ miles long, serving Rhymney and Ebbw Vale. The former made an end on connection with the RR and was the North Western's link to Cardiff. The latter terminated in the centre of Ebbw Vale, from whence a mineral line dropped steeply to the steelworks. The station, with its single platform and small stone building, which was served by a shuttle service from Brynmawr, closed in 1951. Finally there were the two branches from Brynmawr. Running south-east was the Blaenavon branch, opened in 1869 and later extended to Abersychan & Talywain. Running south-west was the Nantyglo branch, opened as late as 1905 by the Brynmawr & Western Valleys Railway. Both terminated in end-on connections with the GWR, which from 1912 for the Blaenavon branch, and 1906 for the Nantyglo branch, worked the passenger services until their respective closures.

The Blaenavon branch commenced with a 2-mile ascent at 1 in 40, which eased just before Waenavon, beyond which the line dropped almost as steeply to Abersychan & Talywain. Waenavon was the summit of the branch, and the highest station on the entire LNWR. At 1400ft this lonely station was the highest in England and Wales. The buildings were of wooden construction and devoid of any awning. This latter omission was probably a shrewd move, for at this height astride a watershed, it is doubtful if such a structure could have withstood the elements for any length of time. Except for a section at the southern end, the branch closed in 1954. However, the section from here to Waenavon was relaid in 1972 by the National Coal Board to serve opencast mine workings. Final closure took place in 1980, and a length remained in place pending possible sale. But now only a short section southwards from the mining museum at Big Pit, Blaenavon, remains for use as a preserved steam railway in conjunction with the adjacent museum.

Fittingly, the last train to use the Merthyr line was a Stephenson Locomotive Society excursion on 5 January 1958, headed by Webb 0–6–2 Coal Tank 58926, now preserved at the Dinting Railway Centre, and G2a 0–8–0 49121. They represented two classes that were the mainstay of the locomotive power for over half a century. How mercilessly those locomotives were worked, although there was no other way with the gradients on these lines. They soon became 'rough' with knocking big-ends, and cracked frames were not uncommon. One can only admire the locomotive staffs at Abergavenny, Tredegar and Blaenavon whose daily task it was to maintain their charges in some semblance of running order. LNWR locomotives earned their reputation for their capacity to be thrashed hard on the Euston to Crewe main line. In this little corner of South Wales their less well-known sisters maintained this tradition in ear-splitting style.

# CHAPTER 5

# Newport

Even today after years of contraction, Newport is the focus of a busy rail network that must be the envy of many larger towns that no longer support a railway of any kind. Its continued usefulness lies in the fact that it was the focal point of no less than five major valley rail networks. Though they have now all lost their passenger services, none until the last decade had lost their railways entirely, although only short lengths remained, as they do this day, in the Rhymney and Sirhowy valleys. During the last few years however, all services have ceased in the Afonlwyd and Ebbw Fach, and these lines, together with the other short sections that have suffered the same fate are described in the Postscript. The Monmouthshire valleys were the first in South Wales to be connected to the sea, via tramroads, between 1805 and 1829. Their growth and prosperity foreshadowed events that were to be repeated in every mining valley as far west as the Gwendraeth in Carmarthenshire. Their metamorphosis to railways was unique in the annals of South Wales' railway history. It must not be forgotten either that Newport and surrounding areas were accustomed to the regular use of the steam locomotive before any other district in South Wales, and before the advent of what we now term as railways. Successful steam haulage first appeared on the Sirhowy tramroad as early as 1829 (an unsuccessful attempt having been abandoned in 1816). The engine did not reach Newport on its first run, but despite this setback steam haulage on the tramroads in the Monmouthshire valleys soon became established. From this time, and for about the next 20 years, locomotive-hauled traffic somehow worked in and around that which was horsedrawn. A local businessman, one John Kingston, was also sufficiently enter-

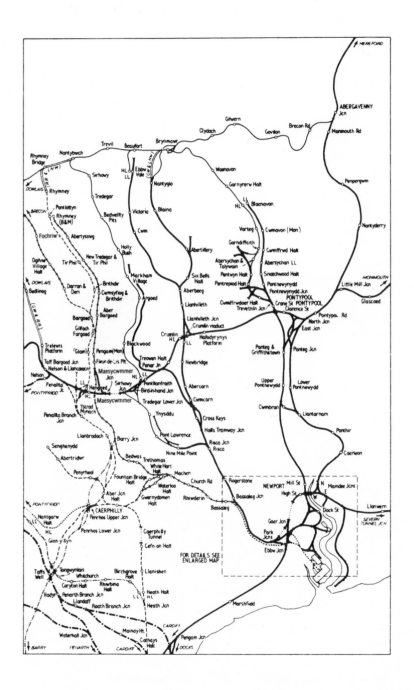

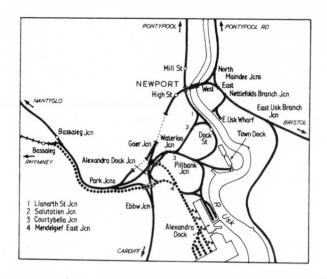

prising to provide a passenger service along the Sirhowy line to
Tredegar as early as 1822, albeit horsedrawn. Within five years
such services had been extended to other major tramroads in
the area.

The first tramroad in Newport was that of the Monmouthshire Railway & Canal Company, or as it was laboriously known
in its Act of 1792 'The Company of the Proprietors of the Monmouthshire Canal Navigation'. In 1805 its tramroad entered
Newport from the Sirhowy Valley, to reach the canal that had
been completed from Ponypool in 1796 and nearby wharves.
This tramroad was, in reality, a continuation of the Sirhowy
Tramroad which had been incorporated on 26 June 1802 to run
from the Tredegar Iron Company's Works to Nine Mile Point
where it joined the Monmouthshire Canal Company's line to
Newport. The Sirhowy was only the third public railway
sanctioned by Parliament. Others of near equal antiquity will be
met later. These were the Carmarthenshire Railway of 3 June
1802, and the Oystermouth Railway of 29 June 1804. These were
respectively the second and fifth public railways.

The Rumney tramroad from the Rhymney Iron Works,
joined the Monmouthshire line from the Sirhowy Valley at Pye
Corner (later known as Bassaleg Junction) from 1826. Three
years later the ironworks at Beaufort and Nantyglo were connected to this system at Risca. From Bassaleg to Newport's

riverside wharves on the Usk, the traffic of these three great iron-works and several lesser ones was carried along a single track by either animal or mechanical motive power. Today it is difficult to visualise how such a system could operate as successfully as it did for over 20 years. In addition to the monies derived from the tolls from this railborne traffic, the Monmouthshire Company owned the canal from Newport to Crumlin and Pontypool. As a result the company ensured that for many years its shareholders were happy and secure. This sense of security was false, for it blinded them to the visions others saw in the asthmatic exhaust beat of those early locomotives. Too late, they and their neighbours in the Sirhowy and Rhymney valleys realised that they must convert themselves into railways. This process finally started in the 1850s and took over a decade to complete. The financial strain of these belated conversions though was too much. For the Monmouthshire Company it drained any resources necessary to fight invaders into its territory, and it gracefully conceded defeat to the Great Western Railway in 1875. The Sirhowy Company, which completed its conversion in 1855, the same year as the Monmouthshire Company, fell to the London & North Western Railway in 1876. With this acquisition, that great railway finally achieved its ambitions of independent entry to South Wales' rich mining valleys, and suitable access to a Bristol Channel port. The last to commence conversion, in 1861, was the Rumney tramroad. It had always been the poor relation in the tramroad network, and the strain of conversion defeated it almost at once. It sold out to the Brecon & Merthyr Railway Company in 1863.

Even then, Newport's rail expansion had yet to reach its peak. This finally came about when the Alexandra Dock Company followed the examples of the Llanelly Dock & Railway Company and the Llynfi & Ogmore Railway by becoming a dock and railway company itself in 1865. Its expansion was not hurried and came about through a nominally independent company, the Pontypridd, Caerphilly & Newport. By 1884 it had succeeded in tapping the riches of the Taff and Rhondda Valleys to Newport, and completed the rail network that once centred on this busy town.

## Newport's Street and Dock Railways

The maritime trade of Newport first developed along the western bank of the river Usk, south of the town bridge. This sheltered tidal stretch once contained over 40 individual wharves, and extended down river to beyond the town's famous transporter bridge. It was fed initially by canal, later supplemented by tramroad and then railway.

This piecemeal riverside development grew out of the fact that the Monmouthshire Company was not a carrier until sometime after 1848. Up to that time freighters supplied their own motive power, to carry their own traffic to their own wharves. Even the opening of the Town Dock in 1842 and the Alexandra Docks in 1875 and 1914 failed to completely kill this riverside trade. To feed these wharves, and the Town Dock, the Monmouthshire Company ultimately developed a railway network, based on the old tramways that gave Newport a street railway network. The later Alexandra Docks (North and South) were fed by their own connecting lines from the Great Western Railway, and by a one-time elevated connection on the western outskirts of the town.

One of the lines of the Monmouthshire's street network is still open, from the site of Courtybella Junction at ST 309871 running south-east then north-east to cross Commercial Street, beyond which it terminates in a coal concentration depot on the site of the former Dock Street station. A one-time continuation of this branch can easily be followed in a south-easterly direction from the site of Pillbank Junction (ST 314869) where the line from Courtybella Junction bears to the north-east. This was the original course of the branch and ran to the Tredegar Wharf, which was built by Homfray & Company for storage and shipping of the output of the Tredegar Ironworks. Its broad course is now part open space and part car park.

A most interesting street line was a part of the first line to enter Newport in 1805. Running from Courtybella Junction, it ran alongside the main Cardiff-Newport Road. Its path can still be seen as a sunken roadway behind trees on the opposite side of the road from Newport's largest hospital, the Royal Gwent.

*Plates 9 and 10.* Special trains. *Above*: An SLS special with ex-GWR 0-6-2T No 6656 at Brynmawr on the former LNWR Merthyr–Abergavenny line. *Below*: No 6656 at Blaenavon (LL), terminus of the former Monmouthshire Railway from Newport. (*Brian Moone*)

Plates *11 and 12*. Interlopers. *Above*: The LNWR at Ebbw Vale High Level station, terminus of the branch that left the Abergavenny–Merthyr line near Beaufort. *Below*: The Midland Railway at Upper Bank in 1959, showing the original Swansea Vale Railway route straight ahead, and the MR line to Morriston and Glais to the left; the locomotive shed can be seen in the fork of the lines. (*Brian Moone, R.O. Tuck*)

Continuing past the hospital, at ST 315875 (outside the offices
of the Transport & General Workers' Union), once known as
Salutation Junction, it divided into two branches. The northernmost branch continued across the Cardiff Road to run along
Kingsway (then known as Ebenezer Terrace) to a junction with
the riverside lines, at the end of Llanarth Street (ST 314879),
across the road from the town's bus station. The southernmost
branch continued along the centre of George Street to join the
riverside lines near Dock Street. These branches were active for
passenger traffic until 1880 and freight until 1907, when the
latter traffic was diverted via Pillbank Junction to Dock Street
and the wharves. Although out of use from 1907 the GWR maintained its right of way along these roadside lines by the annual
passage, on Good Friday, of a locomotive running light. This
ritual continued until 1929 when the GWR disposed of the land
to Newport Corporation.

Of the riverside lines south of the Town bridge none now
remain, save at the George Street coal concentration depot.
From the bridge to the bus station they have disappeared
beneath the road. Beyond, they now lie beneath a car park,
or form the continuation of the main road beyond the bus
station. River traffic still plies to Moderator Wharf in the form
of sand dredgers, and standing on the town bridge as one slips
down river on the tide it is easy to imagine how that river bank
must have bustled with activity. In the early years of this century
such activity kept at least half a dozen locomotives in full employment along the wharves alone during both day and night.

The shed that supplied locomotives for duty in this area was at
Dock Street, which for many years until its closure in 1929 had
a stud of between 50 and 60. Once the main shed and repair
shop for the Monmouthshire Railway, its buildings still stand
today as the premises of a builders' merchant at ST 316872.
Between 1867 and 1876 four passenger and six goods locomotives
were actually built there, thus ensuring for the Monmouthshire
Railway an honour amongst South Wales railways shared only
with the Taff Vale, that of having built its own locomotives.

Mill Street and Dock Street stations were connected along the
riverside from 1855. However, no passenger service ever ran

over these tracks except once in 1927, at a critical stage in the
re-signalling and re-building of High Street station. All traffic
to and from the north was diverted via Waterloo Junction,
Pillbank Junction, Dock Street and Mill Street thence to
Cwmbran and Pontypool and vice versa. For a few glorious
hours, these lines, built to serve the needs of Newport's river
traffic, rang to the sound of GWR passenger locomotives cau-
tiously easing their chocolate-and-cream loads through unfamiliar
territory. Crowds turned out to watch their passage, for it was
not every day that the Great Western ran its expresses along
and across busy roads.

The Monmouthshire Railway's network within Newport was
largely eliminated some years ago, and more recently the
connections and extensive siding networks of the Alexandra
(Newport & South Wales) Dock and Railway Company have
followed their sad demise. As early as 1959 the Park Junction to
Mendalgief East Junction section, connecting Pontypridd to the
docks closed, resulting in the removal of the distinctive overbridge that once crossed the Cardiff Road at ST 298863. Its
distinction lay in the unusual white glazed bricks that faced the
support work. Fortunately a similar bridge built by the same
company still stands at ST 282872, near Bassaleg Junction.

*Newport to Pontypool*

The line from Newport (Mill Street) to Pontypool was built
by the Newport & Pontypool Railway. This Company, actually
the Monmouthshire in disguise, completed its line from Newport
to Pontypool (Crane St) in 1825, and in 1854 connected
end-on with the converted horse drawn tramway to Blaenavon
dating from 1796. Also in 1854 the Newport, Abergavenny &
Hereford Railway made a connection at Coedygric Junction,
south of Pontypool, which brought welcome extra traffic. The
following year saw Mill Street, now the terminus of the Eastern
Valleys traffic, connected to Dock Street, the terminus of the
Western Valleys traffic. This connection was only used for
freight. The line prospered for about 20 years, but on the pro-
jection by the GWR of a parallel line from Newport to Ponty-

pool to relieve the congestion on its Aberdare line, the Monmouthshire Company by now having lost the impetus for railway development in the area, granted the GWR running powers over all its lines and use of all its fixed assets from 1 August 1875. Complete amalgamation took place in 1880. The Great Western completed its line via Caerleon in 1874, and in April 1878 opened a short connecting branch between Llantarnam Junction on the Caerleon line and Cwmbran Junction on the Monmouthshire line. With the opening of this connecting link all passenger traffic into Mill Street ceased in 1880, being diverted into the Great Western High Street station.

Mill Street station was a small affair cramped between the canal on the west and Marshes Road (now Shaftesbury Street) on the east. It only found space to exist at all thanks to a convenient bend in the canal. The initial passenger service to Blaenavon was rather meagre, three up and three down sufficing daily. In 1854 the frequency at Mill Street doubled when the Newport, Abergavenny & Hereford ran its own passenger services between Coedygric and Mill Street. From 1863 the London & North Western also worked into and out of the station, a service which continued intermittently until 1879. With the ever-increasing freight traffic, Mill Street must have presented a very busy and congested appearance. It was probably a relief to the operating authorities when the passenger services were diverted into High Street station.

Since closure in 1966 the inevitable road 'improvements' have destroyed the site of this once busy station, and the approach line from the north as far as its crossing of Shaftesbury Street. Beyond here, though, the line can be followed to the bridge beneath the Newport–Pontypool road. Northwards from here towards the site of Cwmbran Junction roadworks occupy the trackbed. Beyond, the line can be traced to Pontypool. The outstanding engineering features of the line are the hillside shelf, followed by a deep cutting, as it runs through the Crindau and Malpas areas of the town. The former can be seen driving westward along the M4. Approaching the Brynglas tunnel the shelf runs above the eastern portal and can be clearly seen to the north of the motorway. The deep cutting can be seen to advantage at ST 302920 where the line passes beneath the Newport to Pontypool Road (A4042).

As mentioned, passenger services ceased on the Mill St. to Cwmbran Junction section in 1880, and as far as is known no such traffic ever passed over its tracks again, save an SLS special in the 1950s and the day in 1927 when High Street Station was closed. Freight traffic was withdrawn between 1963 and 1967. Mill Street itself finally closed with the closure of the wharfside link to Dock Street on 28 November 1966.

### The Rhymney Valley

The Brecon & Merthyr could have enjoyed the prosperity that came to many of the South Wales railways had it contented itself with its southern section from Dowlais to Newport. However, its very *raison d'être*, to form a link from Mid Wales to the Bristol Channel, was against such a move. Nor could such a move have been made at a later date, due to the continued influence of its Brecon backers on the board. The origin of this southern section of the B&M was the Rumney Railway. This was the last major tramway built in this area, and opened in 1826 from the Rhymney Iron Company's works to a junction with the Monmouthshire Railway at Bassaleg. It sold out to the B&M in 1863, which at that time was still looking for a route to the Bristol Channel, having been thwarted by the other companies in the area.

Almost as impecunious as its purchase, the B&M was obliged to retain almost all of the original alignment of the Rumney line; only in the worst places could any deviation be afforded. In fact, little money was ever available for such improvements, and until its closure this section was always bedevilled by sharp curves. These made operation difficult, and kept the maximum speed down to 40mph (25mph between Aberbargoed and New Tredegar) and with restrictions as low as 15mph in places. The gradients, though, were nowhere as severe over this section. The connection to the northern section was made by running powers for 2 miles 48 chains over the Rhymney Railway from Bargoed South Junction to Deri Junction in the Bargoed Rhymney valley. Here the B&M's own metals were regained for the few steeply-graded miles to Pant, where the original line from Brecon was joined. The battle that took place in this valley is one of the minor classics of Victorian railway history. The problem was the southern entrance to the Bargoed Rhymney. Here nature decreed that a mere defile would open the way to the uplands between the Taff and Rhymney rivers, a defile so narrow that only one line was possible, and which the Rhymney Railway had been given powers to build but which were not exercised. In 1861 the B&M proposed to build along the same alignment. In the fiercely competitive environment of the day the ensuing argument can be imagined. Cool heads eventually prevailed and in the compromise that had to come the Rhymney Railway built the lower section from Bargoed to Deri, and the B&M from there to Pant. Subsequent passenger services, begun in 1868, were only run by the Brecon & Merthyr.

Although the northern section has always held the limelight due to its fearsome gradients and consequent operating practices, it was the southern section that made the profits. Even though the gradients in the narrow Bargoed Rhymney were mainly at 1 in 40 or 1 in 38, they were falling for laden coal trains. Unfortunately these profits could never outweigh the heavy operating expenses of the northern section of the line. Thus the B&M was always the poor relation amongst the railways of the mining valleys.

A most striking example of this relative poverty was that the company never owned any bogie stock, and of the 100 or so coaches taken over by the GWR in 1922 about one-third were 6-wheelers, and the remainder 4-wheeled. Even one of the local colliery companies did better than this by providing bogie stock for its colliers on its workmen's trains. Not only was the B&M stock antiquated, but much was also second-hand, coming from the Mersey Railway and Midland Railway among others. This stock, coupled with its notorious reputation for bad timekeeping, did little to endear the B&M to the travelling public in this area.

Apart from the many sharp curves, from an engineering standpoint the line was typical of its kind, following the eastern side of the Rhymney Valley for much of its course. Unlike the northern section the gradients were uniform, rising continuously towards Rhymney. Following a short initial rise of 1 in 110/82 to just west of Rhiwderin, the ruling gradient was 1 in 234 to a little beyond Maesycwmmer. From there it steepened to 1 in 98/96/99/98 to Rhymney. The only river crossings were on the link to the Rhymney Railway near Bargoed, and at Bassaleg. Here, having left the Rhymney Valley at Machen, the river Ebbw was crossed about a ¼-mile west of the junction with the Western Valleys. For a railway that connected with no fewer than eight others, it was remarkable in the few branches constructed. The ones to Merthyr and Dowlais have already been mentioned, and only one from Machen to Caerphilly was built in the southern section. This added a third river bridge to this portion of the B&M, as will be related later in the chapter.

For anyone who wishes to see the B&M it is pleasant to record that not only does a section still remain in use, as a single-line siding from Bassaleg to Machen, but also that it is still a microcosm of B&M engineering and architecture. Despite daily weekday use some 25 years after the withdrawal of passenger services, more remains of the old B&M in this section than on any part of the abandoned route to Brecon. The only length of equal interest is the Merthyr branch.

Beyond Machen the line can be traced quite easily in many places. It mainly follows a hillside shelf which reaches impressive proportions at ST 153896, where the Barry Railway once crossed the valley on its lofty viaduct to connect with the B&M at Duffryn Isaf. Demolition and road realignments have taken their toll of many interesting features including Maesycwmmer station, which remained with its distinctively-panelled goods shed until about 1972.

Northwards from here the stations at Fleur de Lis and Pengam have been erased, although an overbridge remains at the site of the latter, bearing the inscription 'RUMNEY RAILWAY 1863' and 'EAGLE FOUNDRY CARDIFF'. Only traces of the remaining station platforms can be found as far north as New Tredegar. Here the space between the platform faces now serves as an adventure playground, complete with concrete locomotive. Beyond New Tredegar a landslide forced the closure of the line to Rhymney in 1930. Nearly half a century of disuse, and recent land reclamation in Rhymney itself have now obliterated the B&Ms one-time connection to the Iron Works, the site of which is used by an engineering company. Happily the reclamation work has just missed the Brecon & Merthyr's Rhymney terminus. Its remains can still be seen alongside the Abertwysswg road at SO 121064.

Even though closure took place between Machen and Bedwas in 1986, the essence of this line is distilled into the Bassaleg–Bedwas section. Bassaleg to Machen is typical of the rural B&M whilst from thence to Bedwas the old company's industrial face can still be seen. Leaving the Western Valley line at Bassaleg Junction the line heads westward and soon crosses the Ebbw on a striking stone viaduct, still bearing its date of construction, 1826.

Bassaleg station has long been demolished, together with the goods and locomotive sheds. This latter was a wooden structure, and in 1929 the GWR took a leaf from the book of the thrifty Brecon & Merthyr by dismantling it and re-erecting it at Kidderminster. There it remained until the demise of steam. A mile beyond Bassaleg, Rhiwderin station is passed, now privately-owned. This pleasant building of local stone, together with that at Church Road station, $2\frac{1}{4}$ miles up the valley, typify the rural B&M. Only here and at Brecon, Talyllyn, Talybont and oddly Pengam, did the B&M rise to any height in its station design. Even so, platform awnings were conspicuous by their absence.

Until the summer of 1978 at a point a half-mile beyond Rhiwderin, adjacent to the bridge carrying the A468 over the line, stood the last-remaining B&M signal. Latterly a fixed distant guarding the level-crossing, it had been until about 1968 a working somersault signal. Like all B&M signals, it was similar to those used on the Great Northern Railway, being provided by McKenzie & Holland. Sadly devoid of a finial in its last few years, it stood proudly for 56 years after the extinction of the Brecon & Merthyr. The signalbox that once stood at Rhiwderin and controlled this signal still exists, but not at the station. It now stands at the Caerphilly Railway Society site, in the old locomotive works yard at Caerphilly.

The climb from Bassaleg eases a little beyond here as the

line passes from the Ebbw to the Rhymney Valley. Passing the
secluded station of Church Road, the route ascends and twists its
way along the hillside to Machen Quarry, now the only supplier
of traffic to the line. Beyond, on the now closed section to
Bedwas, the site of the long-disused locomotive works—Machen
Foundry—was passed, and shortly after Machen station, once
the junction for Caerphilly. The buildings that still remain here
are typical of the B&M structures in the industrial areas of the
valley; plain and rendered in cement, its appearance drab. The
line continued to climb along the hillside through the tortured
S-bend of Craig-y-Rhacca curve to the site of Trethomas station.
From here the line was straight for the final 1¼ miles to near the
stop blocks beyond the site of Bedwas station, and actually ran
through the site of the local colliery. From near the stop block site
there is a fine view across the valley, dominated by the ruins of
Caerphilly castle to the south, and the remains of the Barry
Railway's Llanbradach viaduct to the west.

Under Great Western control, the passenger service along
the southern section of the B&M was improved in the 1930s to
six up and seven down trains to and from Rhymney, and five up
and four down to and from Brecon. By this time the old company's stock had been largely replaced by the considerably more
comfortable standard GWR stock. One can only admire the
fortitude of our forefathers who, as late as 1910 were obliged
to travel in 4-wheel stock, with no heating, even in the middle
of winter, and with only the light of dim oil lamps to see by.

### The Connection to the Taff

Understandably, it was normal practice for any railway company
to protect its interests by vehemently attacking any scheme by
a rival company to tap its traffic. The railways of South Wales
were no exception and the annals of Parliament bear mute testimony to these now distant battles. A notable exception occurred
in the relationship between the Taff Vale and the Pontypridd,
Caerphilly & Newport Railways. From the latter's inception
in 1878 relationships were generally cordial, certainly up to
1906. In the PC&N the Taff Vale saw a useful pawn in its

continuous battle of wits with the Bute Dock Company to which it was beholden for access to Cardiff docks, but against whose tolls it continuously complained. A possible alternative shipping outlet was a desirable asset.

The start of this story dates back to 1865 when the Alexandra Dock Company was founded, in opposition to the established Newport Dock Company, and obtained powers to run its own rail system. Connecting railways already tapped the valleys surrounding Newport but unlike the Cardiff Railway some 30 years later, the Alexandra Dock Company wisely decided not to expand in this direction and bring the wrath of the GWR and LNWR down on its head. The traffic of the rich Taff and Rhondda valleys was a different matter, and it was in this direction, through the promotion of the nominally independent Pontypridd, Caerphilly & Newport Railway, that the Alexandra Dock Company expanded. The only possible local opponent was the impoverished Brecon & Merthyr, but the prospect of tolls over its branch from Caerphilly to Machen and thence its main line to Bassaleg, defeated any opposition. For the same reason the prosperous Rhymney Railway did not object to the PC&N traffic travelling between Penrhos Junction and Caerphilly.

The linking of Pontypridd to Newport was accomplished with the minimum of new construction, which opened piecemeal in the years 1884, 1886 and 1891. No continuous line of PC&N metals ever linked these towns, and the company never owned any locomotives, passenger stock, or stations during its independent life, until absorption by the Alexandra (Newport & South Wales) Dock & Railway, as the old dock company was now known, in 1897. The PC&N's method of operation as supplier of a track but not motive power was more akin to the old tramways than that of a railway. However, the revenue it obtained from traffic over its own sections of line must to a large extent have been offset by those which it had to pay to the companies over which its traffic necessarily passed en route to Newport. The only financial winner in such a situation was, of course, the dock company which levied the last toll. The fact that the line existed in separate sections, and that good relations with its neighbours was essential, reflected itself in both mineral, and more particularly passenger services. These latter were complex and unique in South Wales, where at the very least one disdainfully ignored a rival's existence, or more often treated such a rival as a deadly enemy. To describe this fascinating complexity a brief account of the building of the PC&N is necessary.

The first section, from Pontypridd (PC&N Junction) to Penrhos Junction west of Caerphilly, linking the Taff and Rhymney Railways, was opened for mineral traffic in 1884. This allowed through running to Newport even at this date, but access to the Alexandra Dock was via the GWR. The PC&N opened its independent line from Bassaleg to Mendalgief Sidings via Park Junction in April 1886. Now at least the route to Newport began and ended with PC&N metals. The intervening distance was occupied by the Rhymney Railway from Penrhos Junction to Caerphilly, and the Brecon & Merthyr from Caerphilly to Basssaleg. This latter section contained a stretch of 1 in 39 against loaded coal trains, on the single-line branch from Caerphilly to Machen. This difficulty was overcome on 14 September 1891 when the Machen loop line was opened. On a ruling gradient of 1 in 200 against loaded traffic this single line deviated at Gwaunybara Junction and rejoined the original line at Machen Junction. As a point of further complexity, the Machen loop was later transferred to the B&M. We may now come to the traffic operation, on this most singular of systems.

From 1884 to 1906 mineral traffic to Newport was worked by Taff Vale Railway locomotives; during 1906 the A(N&SW)D&R finally started working its own traffic. The passenger services conveniently divide into two types, through and local. The former started at the TVR station in Pontypridd, stopped only at Caerphilly on the Rhymney Railway, and ended at the GWR station in Newport. For exactly eleven years from 28 December 1887 this traffic was worked by the A(N&SW)D&R. From 1 January 1899 it was worked by the GWR until withdrawal as an economy measure on 1 January 1917. It was later reinstated. Local services did not begin until April 1904, and were worked in two independent sections. From Pontypridd to Caerphilly they were worked by the A(N&SW)D&R, but not from the TVR station. That company refused entry for such traffic, so services began and ended on the Newport Company's own metals at Tram Road Halt. At this time the GWR-worked through services were allowed to use the TVR station, as had the similar services of the Newport Company been so allowed up to six years before! The *crème de la crème* of these local services occurred on the B&M section between Caerphilly and Machen. This section had such services provided neither by the B&M (who owned the metals), or the A(N&SW)D&R (who ostensibly worked the traffic), but by the Rhymney until 1919, the Newport company at last having worked its own local services as far as Machen from 1917 after the GWR's withdrawal. Even now this company's idiosyncrasies were not over. Two more may be recalled; firstly all the stations owned by the A(N&SW)D&R were confined to the original Pontypridd to Penrhos section, and that the wide separation of the lines between Gwaunybara Junction and Machen resulted in separate halts being established on both lines, but which could only be served by trains from one direction only.

With all the possible traffic permutations involving so many companies one can only sympathise with the inhabitants of Rudry, a small village between Cardiff and Machen. As soon as through passenger services started in 1887, they petitioned for a station or halt near Gwaunybara (later the junction of the Machen Loop), but had to wait until 1908 before such a halt was opened. One can easily realise the reasons for delay. The through services were run by the Alexandra Dock Railway, originally on behalf of the PC&N, then taken over by the GWR. Such services were over tracks of the B&M Company. Finally the local services were, during the latter part of the 20-year wait, worked by the Rhymney Railway. Thank heaven that no other part of South Wales ever reached such complexity.

### The Sirhowy Valley

Up to its closure the Sirhowy branch gave to Newport the distinction of being the only GWR main line station in South Wales to which the LMS ran. Here over the years, at the back of the station, the black and red products of Webb, Bowen-

Cooke, Fowler and Stanier could be compared (usually dero-
gatorily) with the green products of Dean, Churchward, Collett
and Hawksworth. For the LMS to reach its own metals, traffic
from High Street station ran via the GWR to Risca and thence
to Nine Mile Point. This latter place, which formed an end-on
junction between the two companies, was so named as it was
originally nine miles from the end of the Monmouthshire Railway's tramroad from Newport. It marked the start of the
Sirhowy Railway, which sold out to the London & North
Western Railway in 1876. Incidentally, the running of traffic
from the Sirhowy over the Monmouthshire's tramroad from
1805 must be the first example in the world of the granting of
running powers between railways.

The acquisition of the Sirhowy Railway by the LNWR and its
subsequent integration into that company's network set this line
apart from its neighbours. Even in LMS days its origins were
unmistakable. They were daily proclaimed to the sky by the
distinctive LNWR-style signals. As elsewhere on that railway
they could never make up their minds how much their arms
should drop (the GWR signal arm drop of 45° was much more
positive), and their flat finials always looked like an afterthought.
They were certainly built to last, for they outlived the LNWR,
the LMS, and integration into the Western Region of British
Railways, until finally felled some years after closure. The last,
at Pontllanfraith, succumbed in the early 1970s. When one talks
of signals, signalboxes come to mind, and these also proclaimed
that they belonged to Euston and not Paddington. Nine Mile
Point No 1 was typical of the breed. Hemmed in between the
railway and the river, it was a rather tall and slender wooden
signalbox with a steeply-pitched roof typical of LNWR style.
Its name was proudly proclaimed above the door at the top of
a steep flight of steps, fixed parallel to the running lines. Inside
the lever frame was narrower and taller than its GWR counter-
part, and to my mind not as easy to operate.

Nine Mile Point station itself was an oddity that could only
be called into being thanks to the one-time intricacies of the
British railway system. It existed solely to mark the division
between the LNWR and GWR sections in the valley. No village

of that name exists, nor is there a village within easy reach. To be true, Bradshaw at one time sought to regularise the position by indicating that it was the station for Upper Machen, $1\frac{1}{2}$ miles away on the B&M system. Unfortunately, it failed to inform the traveller that he had to climb over a mountain of 1192ft to reach it. Even the station layout was a little unusual. The platforms were staggered, and joined by a level-crossing between their extremities. The only station building was on the up side. This consisted of a single-storey wooden structure, typically LNWR, and for many years the station master maintained a trim hedge behind it. His large house was nearby, part of the outbuildings of which had been stables, for in tramroad days horses were changed here as traffic passed to and from the Sirhowy system. Two signalboxes once existed here, a GWR one at the south end, and a LNWR one at the north end; as a consequence up and down starting signals were LNWR and GWR respectively.

In gradients and bends the line was much like its neighbours. Gradients were between 1 in 88 and 1 in 150 as far as Tredegar, but steepened to 1 in 42 for the two miles of single line to the isolated junction of Nantybwch, where Sirhowy branch trains had their own bay platform. The lower part of the valley was less despoiled than many others and the scenery quite picturesque, being thickly wooded in places. Even in the upper reaches of the valley such beauty was not allowed to be forgotten, even if industrial pollution was dominant. For many years the small station at Hollybush sported potted plants and hanging baskets, which made this station a little gem.

The most important intermediate station was at Pontllanfraith, formerly known as Tredegar Junction. Here the GWR Pontypool–Neath line passed beneath the Sirhowy branch, and made connection at Bird-in-Hand Junction. The name was taken from that of a local public house, which happily still serves its customers, unlike the junction. Just to the south was a further connection, Sirhowy Junction to Tredegar Lower Junction (of LNWR ownership), completion of which enabled traffic interchange in all directions between the two lines. These connections were very important, since for many years the GWR used running powers to enable its traffic from the Aberdare and other

valleys to reach the South of England by a shorter and less
steeply graded route than through Pontypool. It also used these
running powers for some years prior to World War I to run a
railmotor service from Newport to Merthyr via Quaker's Yard
and the Merthyr Joint Line. This service did not call at any
LNWR stations.

It was not until after World War II that LNWR motive power
gave way to standard LMS designs. For decades the mainstays
of the line were Webb's 0–6–2 Coal Tanks, and the G2 0–8–0s,
together with the massive Bowen-Cooke 0–8–4Ts. In later years
Stanier Class 3 and Ivatt Class 2 2–6–2Ts came to the line,
before finally being displaced in the last years, on passenger
workings, by the ubiquitous GWR pannier tank. LMS locomotives worked the freight traffic though throughout. Passenger
rolling stock was more varied, and the LNWR's hold was relin-
quished sooner. By the mid-1930s Lancashire & Yorkshire and
Furness Railway stock were much in evidence. Even some new
LMS stock was provided at this time, and when excursions
headed north for Wales vs Scotland rugby internationals saloon
stock was provided. Although isolated from their main system,
both the LNWR and LMS never forgot the importance of this
branch.

# CHAPTER 6

# Cardiff and Barry

In 1834 the Customs Officer of Cardiff, which at that time was little more than a village at the head of a navigable inlet, wrote in his annual report, "No coal can ever be raised within this Port in order to be shipped for exportation or be carried coastwise, its distance from water rendering it too expensive for any such sale." His successor was equally adamant, for a few years later, when the first dock was being built, he reported, "We have no coals exported from this Port, nor ever shall, as it would be too expensive to bring it down from the internal part of the country."

The first rail link, from "the internal part of the country", was completed in 1841, and coal exports commenced almost immediately. In 50 years Cardiff had become one of the greatest ports in the United Kingdom, and the village had grown to a fine city.

The pioneer railway was the Taff Vale, running from Merthyr. In the same period it became one of the most prosperous of railways, with dividends once reaching $17\frac{1}{2}\%$. The phenomenal industrial growth of this area led, just after the turn of the 20th century, to Cardiff playing host to no fewer than six independent railway companies. For a decade the Taff Vale Railway was alone, until the broad gauge South Wales Railway entered in 1850. This was later to become the Great Western Railway's main line in South Wales, being absorbed by the GWR in 1863, and converted to standard gauge in 1872. However, it was connected to the Taff Vale Railway from 1854 by a mixed-gauge connection, following an unsuccessful attempt to persuade the Taff Vale to convert its gauge to 7ft 0 in.

The third member of this sextet was the Rhymney Railway Company, which in 1857 completed an isolated branch from the

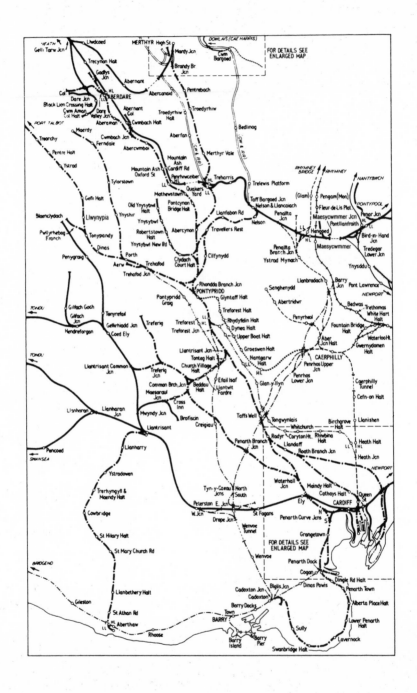

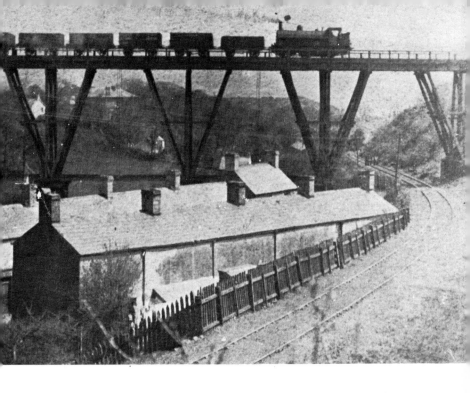

*Plates 13 and 14.* Timber trestles–the Dare Viaduct. *Above*: A view taken in the early years of the 20th century. The line in the foreground is the TVR Bwllfa–Dare branch. *Below*: The viaduct in 1946, shortly before demolition. (*Cynon Valley Library, Glyn Davies*)

Plates 15 and 16. Contrasts in motive power. *Above*: GWR 2-4-2T No 3605 at Mountain Ash (Cardiff Road) in 1905. *Below*: LMS Class 2 2-6-0 No 46507 and ex-GWR 0-6-0PT No 3638 at Brecon. (*Cynon Valley Library, Brian Moone*)

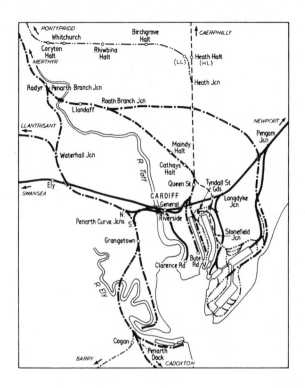

Taff Vale Railway to the newly-opened East Dock. Its main line eventually connected with this branch some 14 years later, entry previously having been over Taff Vale metals by exercise of running powers. In the same year the LNWR also gained access to Cardiff, with the opening of its joint line with the Rhymney Company between Nantybwch and Rhymney. Simultaneously it opened its own independent line within the Cardiff dock area.

Demands for more port facilities, and a breaking of the transport monopoly from the rich valleys held by the TVR brought about in 1884 the incorporation of the Barry Railway, combined with its own docks at Barry. This was the last major railway to penetrate the coalfield in this area. It was this company which later, at the height of its phenomenal expansion, won against bitter opposition, was referred to as "the spoilt child of Parliament". By this time it already tapped or threatened to tap the coal trade of every port from Newport to Swansea. As part of its expansionist policies it reached Cardiff in 1893, having obtained running powers over the TVR and GWR.

The sixth and last entrant into Cardiff was the Cardiff Railway. In 1897 it obtained powers to build its own connecting lines to the docks, but only one was ultimately constructed. From Heath Junction on the Rhymney Railway it ran to join the TVR at Treforest, and was completed in 1909. However, the TVR was successful in preventing the junction from ever being used. As a result, the Cardiff Railway never grew beyond a local branch.

Of these lines that once entered Cardiff, only the older ones have survived in any substantial form. The Taff Vale and Rhymney lines, shorn of some branches and having lost a large amount of passenger traffic, still survive. The old GWR main line is still viable. The LMS (as successor to the LNWR) ceased operation in the docks in the early 1930s. The two late arrivals have fared worst. The Barry system has been decimated, only branches to Bridgend and Cardiff survive. The Cardiff Railway is now a single-track commuter line from Heath Junction to Coryton Halt, on the city's northern outskirts.

### In the Valleys

Within the valleys the Taff Vale Railway's system, which was basically completed between 1840 and 1860, remains essentially intact, as does that of the Rhymney Railway. The lines of their one time competitors have suffered total annihilation, as already described in earlier chapters; and as will be described in the next, the Taff Vale's branches to the south-west outside the Taff valley, the construction of which occupied the years 1863–1892 are rapidly fading memories.

Many of the closures of TVR and RR branches are of small sections of line, or have occurred only recently, and will be found in The Postscript. But the closure of many important sections of the TVR took place some years ago, and were of a number of branches each with unique characteristics.

That of the Blaenrhondda branch, opened in the summer of 1878, was that it was to have been the start of a line linking the Taff Vale to the Vale of Neath Railway at Hirwaun, under the auspices of the Rhondda Valley & Hirwaun Junction Railway.

This grandiose scheme foundered a little beyond Blaenrhonnda colliery, at the foot of the precipitous slopes that dominate the head of the Rhondda Fawr. Standing on the close-cropped sheep-grazed trackbed of this line, one wonders at the temerity of the promoters in thinking about such a scheme as a tunnel to Hirwaun, but only a mile away is the bricked-up tunnelling masterpiece of the Rhondda & Swansea Bay Railway. The task would not have been impossible, just expensive. The Rhondda & Swansea Bay only succeeded since it needed to tap the riches of the Rhondda. The Taff Vale would have found it useful to have had a direct western outlet of its own from this valley, but it did not need it. To tackle such formidable obstacles as the mountains separating the Welsh Valleys, one had to have an urgent need with no alternatives.

One might be forgiven for thinking that lines built purely for mineral exploitation, and of relatively short length, would exhibit little in the way of interest. The pretentions of the Blaenrhondda branch have just been mentioned, and two others each displayed a unique individuality. One contained throughout its long life which stretched into the middle of this century that operator's nightmare, a rope-worked incline. The other was built essentially in three parts, serving one terminus, and having two main-line junctions. It also had an incline in its early years.

## The Pwllyrhebog Branch

This branch was justly famous for its fearsome 1 in 13 incline, and also, that for some 67 out of the 82 years of the line's existence, work on the incline itself was performed by a unique trio of specially designed 0–6–0Ts, TVR Class H Nos 141–3 (GWR Nos 792–4). They worked alone from 1884 until about 1915, when the first of a series of conventional tank engines was sent to assist them, every one of which, except the last, they outlived. The branch was built in 1863 to serve the Blaenclydach colliery, and was joined in 1889 by a private line (acquired by the TVR in 1896) from the Clydach Vale Colliery.

Throughout its entire life, locomotives worked on the incline. In the *Appendix to the Service Timetable* $1\frac{1}{2}$ pages, containing

11 instructions for the incline alone, were needed for this branch. Among these, the following are noteworthy:

1. This incline is worked by two engines and attached to a wire rope. One engine passes Up and Down on the left hand line and the other on the right hand line. The rope must be attached to both engines when they are running on the Incline.

2. Under all circumstances the engine must be at the bottom or Pwllyrhebog end of the wagons.

4. The maximum number of wagons authorised for each run is Ten empties or Five wagons of pitwood Up and Ten loaded 12-ton wagons or Six loaded 20-ton wagons Down.

6. The speed of the engines, with or without wagons, must not exceed Five miles per hour on any part of the Incline.

Prior to 1884 it was Taff Vale practice to use old locomotives due for scrap on the incline, but it became an increasing nuisance to have to keep changing the haulage equipment. Hence in 1884 the company supplied specially-designed locomotives to work the incline, and the steeply-graded line beyond; these were to survive until the line closed. The locomotives, 0–6–0Ts, had specially-designed boilers steeply tapered because of the gradient, and were carried on wheels of 5ft 3in diameter. These were unusually large for shunters, and were in fact a standard size at that time for Taff Vale passenger locomotives. The reason for their use was that with counterbalancing assistance, power was not of major importance, and large-diameter wheels gave ample clearance for the haulage gear. The locomotives were built by Kitson & Co and were delivered in December 1884. A shed was built near the top of the incline to house them, but they were officially allocated to Treherbert. Usually two worked the branch, each being used for four weeks with two weeks off. Sometime during 1915 their load was shared by assisting locomotives as mentioned, thus enabling the branch locomotives to work in pairs, two weeks on and two weeks off, until closure on 1 July 1951. Before leaving this unique trio it must be mentioned that none of them ever visited Swindon during their working lives. However the former No 142, as GWR No 194, was cut-up there after withdrawal in 1953, unrebuilt from Taff Vale days. Even Collett could not standardise this trio.

Coal was not the only produce to pass up and down this branch. Blaenclydach boasted a goods station and yard, with facilities for handling livestock. In fact, there were few restrictions on the type of wagons that could ascend to Blaenclydach. 'Well' vehicles were the only ones prohibited, owing to clearance problems with the winding sheaves.

## The Nelson Branch

At the turn of the century the Taff Vale Railway was in the middle of a great expansion of passenger traffic, an expansion in part forced on it by competition from the Barry Railway. Its endeavours to date had been successful, and flushed by this success it started a service in June 1900 from Pontypridd via Pont Shon Norton Junction up the eastern side of the Taff Valley to Nelson. The service never flourished, and a look at a map indicates why. Its most populated area was so close to Pontypridd that non-railway transport was much more convenient, and at Nelson, the village's needs were much better serviced by the Nelson & Llancaiach station of the GWR. Determined efforts were made to stimulate traffic, and the branch saw the early introduction of railmotors, that peculiar hybrid of steam locomotive and carriage extensively used by the TVR. The service survived until September 1932, when the northern end of the branch was closed. Latterly the weekday-only service consisted of six trains each way. The journey time was 19 minutes to Nelson from Pontypridd, and 18 minutes in the reverse direction. These timings were beaten on Saturday nights when the 11.23pm to Pontypridd ran non-stop in 14 minutes. Despite the A470 by-pass, Pontypridd is still notorious for congestion, and 14 minutes from Nelson to Pontypridd 56 years after the last service would still take some beating.

The history of this line would perhaps have been different if Parliament had passed in its entirety the Rhymney Railway Company's Bill of 1854, which made provision to connect with the Taff Vale at Llancaiach, and not at Walnut Tree Junction. Connection was eventually made in 1858 to the Newport, Abergavenny & Hereford Railway Taff Vale Extension for goods only, but it brought little traffic to the branch, the vast majority of traffic passing the junction being for GWR outlets.

As originally built, the branch deviated from the main line at Stormstown Junction, headed north-east across the valley on an embankment, and crossed the river on a substantial four-arched stone bridge, sadly now demolished. It then ascended the hillside by a rope-worked incline, before turning south-east, about 1¼ miles beyond the incline top, towards Nelson. It is puzzling that despite his lack of interest in the line, and the need for economy in its construction, Brunel favoured a stone bridge over the river here, and elsewhere, instead of his famous timber ones. Eventually the incline was abandoned, and a new line laid from its foot to join the original one just before it turned south-eastwards. Finally in 1887, a new line was made just north of Pontypridd to serve the Albion colliery at Cilfyndd; this was extended northwards three years later to join the Nelson branch, thus giving it a second junction with the main line. For a small mineral line that missed its chances, to have been built in three parts and to have had two junctions with the main line is rather remarkable. The remains of the incline and the upper part of the original branch are clearly visible today. The view from the incline top is magnificent and historically of great interest. Here one is almost directly above the long-vanished terminal of the Penydarren tramway, on which the steam age started.

### The Barry Railway

It is an odd twist of fate that the only thriving part of the old Barry Railway system is the once financially embarrassing line to Bridgend, now forming a vital link for coal traffic to Aberthaw Power Station. The main line of the Barry Railway, which in its peak year of 1913 hauled more than 11 million tons of coal for export at Barry Docks is now a memory, for while in the heyday of the South Wales coalfield it performed the vital function of hauling the embarrassment of riches to the sea, it was a parasite of a railway. It served few collieries direct, its riches were obtained by deftly abstracting, from July 1889, a vast amount of traffic from the already well-established lines in the area. A measure of these riches can be gauged from the fact that in one year the dividend fell to only 6%. At this the shareholders threatened revolt, changes were made, and for the last ten years of the company's existence it never went below $9\frac{1}{2}$%.

I well recall trips from Cardiff to Barry Island in the immediate post-war period. On leaving Cadoxton station I never ceased to be amazed at the extensive layout to both right and left. On the right the main line swept in between immense fans of sidings. The layout here was so complex that drivers had to know no less than 33 whistle codes to communicate with the signalmen. (In all, 142 whistle codes were in use in the dock area.) On the left was the great expanse of running lines, loops, sidings and coal hoists along the northern sides of the two docks. Coal wagons both full and empty were everywhere, in stark contrast to the present day scene, although the bulk of the coal at that time was being imported rather than exported.

Barry Island as a pleasure resort owes its existence to the enterprise of the Barry Railway and its successor the GWR, which developed it as a holiday centre between the two World Wars. From Barry Island station a short branch ran through a tunnel beneath the headland, and out onto the landing stage at Barry Pier. The branch was used to connect with the company's steamers, known as the Red Funnel fleet, which ensured for the company the distinction of being numbered among that select band of railways that ran their own steamer services. No regular services ever ran on this branch, only those in conjunction with the steamers. The line closed even to this limited traffic in 1971. The station site overlooking the entrance to the harbour can still be seen, and is now largely used by a local yacht club.

The Barry main line was totally different in character to its neighbours, for it had to fight its way through the hill country

to the west of the Taff Valley to achieve its objective. Beyond
Wenvoe station, a delightful red brick structure now owned by a
local agricultural firm, the builders met their first serious
obstacles. From here on the heavy engineering started. The first
example was the Wenvoe tunnel, over a mile long, and one of
the longest in South Wales. Beyond, the first connection (the
Drope branch), dropped away westwards to the GWR main
line. The main line now continued northwards, spanning the
Ely Valley by a pair of handsome stone viaducts. These fine
structures, demolished in October 1981, were an impressive
monument to the railway builders of the 19th Century.

East of this viaduct, on the South Wales main line, once stood
St Fagans station, and it was from here that the Barry built a
branch to connect with its own main line. The Barry company
was extremely enterprising in its provision of passenger services.
Among these, the rival service over this steep and sharply-curved
branch between Cardiff and Pontypridd, against the Taff Vale,
ranks as the most enterprising. It was a local wonder that it
survived for so long. It commenced in 1896 with a service of
ten trains each way daily, and was not finally withdrawn until
1962. Latterly motive power was supplied by a 64xx class 0-6-0
pannier tank hauling a single auto coach. Such was the affection for this cheeky little warrior and its predecessors that used
to pound along the main line from Cardiff and up into the hill
country to reach Pontypridd the long way around, that it earned
itself the nickname of 'The St Fagans Pullman'.

Heavy civil engineering work continued as the line progressed,
culminating in a wide shelf cut into the western slopes bordering the Taff Valley, together with a steeply descending connection to the Taff Vale Railway. It eventually emerged in the outskirts of Pontypridd, at its own station on the hill above the Taff
Vale's, and finally forced its way to the Rhondda Valley, to make
its last connection at Trehafod.

The Barry's final expansion, which commenced in 1896,
tapped the Rhymney and Brecon & Merthyr systems from
Tyn-y-Caeau Junction. The line was difficult to build and expensive, but it was one of the most spectacular lines built in this area.
It was a line that literally clawed its way forward by cutting,

tunnel, hillside shelf, and viaduct after viaduct to its goal. To understand why such an expensive and spectacular route was followed, visualise the scene that once unfolded from the Barry's Walnut Tree viaduct, near Taffs Well. Looking down 120ft to the valley floor, the reason could clearly be seen. The Nantgarw gap is only a few hundred yards wide, and has precipitous sides. West to east beneath, were a minor road, a private railway, the river, the Taff Vale Railway's main line, the Glamorganshire Canal, and the main road to Merthyr. The small gap between this road and the eastern cliff was already earmarked for the Cardiff Railway. On the valley floor there was nowhere for the Barry to go. For some 60 years that scene changed little, but during the last decade the change has been drastic. The viaduct, apart from its western abutment and one pier, the private railway, the original main road, the canal, and the Cardiff Railway have all disappeared. The last three are now buried beneath the new Cardiff–Merthyr road.

Wherever the Barry went along this route, its rivals held the best ground. As a result two more viaducts had to be built before it could reach the Rhymney, and Brecon & Merthyr systems north of Caerphilly.

At its peak mineral traffic was immense. No less than 80 to 90 coal trains were booked from Trehafod, Treforest, the Rhymney Valley and Peterston daily in the down direction. That was, on average, one loaded coal train every 16 minutes along the main line between Wenvoe and Cadoxton. It was as well that the area traversed was sparsely populated, and that six trains each way daily sufficed for passenger needs. In fact, this level of passenger service was maintained throughout much of the line's life. The only regular passenger service to work over the Rhymney Valley branch was during the period 1924–1932 (summer timetable only). This was a through working from Pontypool Road to Barry Island via Ystrad Mynach, Penrhos Junction and Tyn-y-Caeau Junction. However, from early days excursion trains running from the LNWR (later LMS) in the Tredegar area used it. Motive power, latterly at least, was provided by ex-LNWR G2 0–8–0s, many with tender cabs.

## *The Penarth—Cadoxton Branch*

Stung, or perhaps more truthfully, caught on the wrong foot, by the aggressiveness of a prospective competitor, the Taff Vale Railway sought to contain the threat in the Penarth area by proposals to build not one, but two lines between Penarth and Barry. After much horse-trading, it managed to obtain powers in 1885 to build only one of these lines. This was the longer but more heavily graded coastal line, scenically superior but potentially less profitable. On reflection it got the worst of the deal.

It is for day trips to Lavernock that I remember this forgotten branch. I will always associate it with the long sunny days of childhood, crowded carriages, and the mile walk to the beach. Until finally defeated by the car this was the branch of the holidaymaker. Lavernock station stood adjacent to the road leading to the beach, high on an embankment on its eastern side. Today it is almost impossible to imagine the queues that used to form in late summer afternoons. They would start at the top of the narrow path leading down from the platform, tail back down to the road, and continue beneath the skew bridge for up to 50yd or more towards the beach at St Mary's Well Bay. When the platform was eventually gained, one was confronted with excursions comprised of non-corridor stock already heaving with humanity. The subsequent journeys too were also memorable for the sight and sound of the old tank engines struggling noisily up the gradient to Penarth Town.

Built as a competitive line, the company spared little in expenditure, giving it the most delightful appearance of any of its lines. Buildings of grey stone, with yellow-brick window and door frames, blended harmoniously with their surroundings in a way never achieved before by this railway. Alas, through being much longer and more heavily graded its efforts were not crowned with success. It never realised the freight or passenger traffic hoped for. It lived on its commuter traffic to Penarth, which was actively developed and supplemented by summer holiday traffic. The only staple freight was supplied by the cement works east of Lavernock.

The closure of the branch beyond Penarth followed the

familiar pattern of reduced services, withdrawal of facilities, and
the closure of one of the halts. Since 1968 Penarth Town station
has reverted to its original status as a terminus. The buildings
on the down platform are now in private hands, and on the site
of the goods yard stands a trim modern housing estate. The goods
shed at Lavernock produces electronic equipment, and whilst
Sully's once attractive station has ceased to exist, enterprising
local horticulturalists have successfully grown strawberries up the
side of the nearby cutting. Nowadays people no longer queue
along the road to St Mary's Well Bay—only cars.

## The Cardiff Railway

The ex-Rhymney Railway tank engine wheezed and clanked
out of the sidings at Nantgarw colliery at the head of some three
dozen coal wagons, destined for the Steel Company of Wales at
Margam. Crossing and re-crossing the Cardiff–Pontypridd road
it picked up speed, and began a gentle run down the eastern side
of the valley. In sight of the tracks of its once bitter enemy, it
trundled south towards the Nantgarw gap. Here, as the valley
narrowed, it crossed the canal and ducked beneath the old
Rhymney line from Penrhos Junction. Immediately afterwards,
and dwarfed by the towering Walnut Tree Viaduct, it squeezed
itself between cliff and road, on an embankment retained by a
red brick wall, and whistling shrilly disappeared into the short
tunnel north of Tongwynlais station. Soon afterwards this derelict site was passed, and the locomotive eased its load around
the long curve to the east and headed towards Heath Junction.

Such was the scene in the early 1950s on the former Cardiff
Railway, some 42 years after its opening. It was the long-delayed
heyday of the line, and it was its swan song. This activity only
lasted until 1952, when the Western Region made a new connec-
tion to the ex-Taff Vale line just north of Taffs Well station.
This too has now closed following the passing of Nantgarw
Colliery in 1986; the line to Coryton Halt having closed in 1952.
Beyond here it remains open handling commuter traffic only.

Born from the reconstituted Bute Dock Company, which had
become the Cardiff Railway Company in 1897, it sought at the

turn of the century to have its own personal railway to bring traffic to its docks. Spurred on by the success of the Barry Railway, it built its line from Heath Junction on the Rhymney Railway, west and then north through the Nantgarw gap to join the Taff Vale, just south of its Treforest Station. From here it hoped to tap from that railway traffic from the Taff, Rhondda and Cynon Valleys, as the Barry Railway had done so successfully. Naturally the Taff Vale was not amused. It had fought unsuccessfully for a number of years to stop the Barry bleeding-off a considerable proportion of its traffic. Now it was totally successful over a period of some 13 years in preventing the Cardiff Railway from ever taking any coal traffic from it at Treforest. The only train to make use of the junction was the inaugural train in 1909.

Bravely, goods and passenger traffic were commenced between Cardiff and Rhydyfelin, making use of the Rhymney's Cardiff station as its southern terminus. Not surprisingly freight traffic did not develop as was anticipated. However, by way of compensation, a healthy passenger traffic developed over the southern portion of the line as Cardiff expanded. The line managed to survive intact until 1931, when it was closed to passenger traffic north of Coryton Halt. Its Indian Summer came with the opening of the Nantgarw Colliery shortly after World War II, but it was short-lived. Today only a commuter service continues to Coryton. Beyond, few traces remain from here to Glanllyn, and the only visible evidence north of Nantgarw is on the west bank of the Taff. Here the embankment at Treforest junction and the bridge abutment remain.

### Within the City

Apart from their lines to the coalfields, the local companies had branches within the City. These lines were links to the docks or its immediate surroundings but were not, with one exception, part of the dockside railway system.

### The Roath Branch

This was the longest of this group of forgotten lines, being built by the Taff Vale Railway in 1888 to feed directly the newly opened Roath dock. Double-tracked throughout, it diverged to the east about a ½-mile south of Llandaff station. Immediately it ran into a broad deep cutting, flanked to the south by extensive sidings. Beyond, it curved south towards the dock area, and for much of its remaining length was on an embankment. Its most noteworthy engineering features were the series of bridges which once spanned the Cardiff–Newport Road, the South Wales main line, and finally a group of now defunct sidings. These bridges have been removed in piecemeal fashion over recent years. A peculiar operating feature of the branch was that it was permitted to run two coal trains along it coupled together, provided the load did not exceed 80 wagons down or 60 wagons up.

Originally running along the boundary of the fast growing city, it later became part of today's inner suburbs. As a by-product of Cardiff's growth, one of its most beautiful parks was developed immediately north of the line, about a mile from its junction. Here it was possible, whilst wandering through superb rose gardens, to watch an almost continuous procession of export traffic. Today the embankment still remains, widened, and now a part of Cardiff's inner relief road. The coal traffic it once carried is now gone, but at least the roses are still there to enjoy.

### The East Dock Branch

This branch, 1¼ miles long, was built by the Rhymney Railway in 1857, on a series of embankments and bridges, between Crockherbtown Junction and Roath Dock. It was the oldest forgotten branch within the city. The Rhymney's original Cardiff terminus stood on it at Adam Street until 1871, when it became a goods depot. An interesting feature here, was the working of the 'Old Coal Yard'. This yard was at street level, and connected to the depot by a steep inclined siding. To lower a wagon, a rope was attached between it and the locomotive; when taut, the locomotive moved forward, lowering the wagon. Two loaded 10-ton wagons only could be lowered at a time, whilst four empties could be raised. This branch died after more than a century of groaning beneath the weight of innumerable coal wagons that once streamed, full and empty, in continuous procession along it. These were propelled by generations of over-worked tank engines. It died, unnoticed and unsung.

Rather interesting is the fate of the site of the northern approach to the goods depot, and the adjacent sidings of the Taff Vale Railway along the eastern side of their Queen St. station, which once shared the same elevated site. On them stands the towering office block, Brunel House, once British Rail's South Wales headquarters, and originally destined in fact to fulfil that function for the entire Western Region.

## The Tyndall Street Branch

This was the shortest line, and a totally isolated part of the London & North Western Railway empire. Only 45 chains in length, it was built in 1875. In the heart of Cardiff's dockland, it ran north and then west from a junction at the end of the Rhymney's East Dock branch, to a three-storey warehouse at Tyndall Street. To reach it the LNWR used its running powers over the Rhymney system from Nantybwch. The importance that the LNWR attached to this outlet can be realised by considering that in the early years of this century it worked as many as five down and six up goods trains daily, into and out of Cardiff docks. It used its own locomotives for these trains; in addition, for shunting, it maintained an 0–6–2T permanently stationed at the Rhymney's East Dock shed. After absorption into the LMS, its locomotives still continued to run to Cardiff, and were later supplemented by Midland Railway Class 4 0–6–0s. These services continued until 1933, when a traffic pooling agreement between the GWR and LMS terminated the latter's through locomotive workings.

## The Riverside Branch

This was the busiest branch. Just under a mile long, it had been constructed from a point just west of Cardiff Station to the docks area by the GWR in 1882. At that time it was for freight only. It was rebuilt some ten years later for passenger traffic. Oddly, the GWR never ran a passenger service over it until after the grouping. From 1894 this service was maintained jointly by the Barry and Taff Vale Railways. Goods traffic was always worked by the GWR, which it somehow fitted around the intensive passenger service. The terminus was at Clarence Road in the heart of what was the business centre of the city, near the Coal Exchange. Additionally, the GWR built platforms complete with separate booking offices, on the branch, adjacent to their station. At the General Manager's suggestion, these platforms were named Riverside Junction station. Why this suggestion was made is a mystery, since these platforms were so obviously a part of the main station. This state of affairs continued until rebuilding took place in the 1930s. Riverside Junction station became platforms 8 and 9 of Cardiff General (now Central) station. Since the closure of the branch in 1964 they have been used for parcels traffic.

The passenger service was intense for over 40 years. The Barry started the services in 1894 with 17 trains each way daily. Ever enterprising in its cultivation of traffic it later graced the branch, in the summer of 1906, with a named train. This was the 'Ilfracombe Boat Express', which it ran in conjunction with its steamer services. The 'express' ran non-stop from Cardiff to Barry Pier station. By 1907, with the Taff Vale also firmly established, the daily total of services had risen to 40 each way daily, 10 of which maintained the Barry's competitive Pontypridd service via St Fagans. In addition Riverside station was handling a further 17 trains a day terminating, and a similar number starting, from there. Thus the branch was handling no less than 114 passenger or empty stock workings daily. This flood continued unabated until the 1930s. In fact the overall level was unaltered in 1932. Only the balance of traffic, to numerous destinations, had altered slightly.

Even at this period, though, the decline of Cardiff as a shipping and commerce centre was under way, and this level of railway activity could not be sustained. The area of Cardiff that this branch served is now dead as such a centre, and with its death the line too has passed away.

# CHAPTER 7

# Bridgend and Llantrisant

As befitted what was a mainly agricultural region, the first railway intrusion into the Vale of Glamorgan was appropriately horse-powered. This forerunner first appeared when the Dyffryn Llynfi & Porthcawl Railway opened in 1828 to haul coal from the Dyffryn Colliery to a harbour at Porthcawl. A connecting tramway from near Tondu to Bridgend (the Bridgend Railway) was opened two years later. For 20 years they held the monopoly of rail transport in the area, until the South Wales Railway in 1850 opened its line through Bridgend. Another five years elapsed before sufficient local support could be found to convert these tramroads into steam-hauled railways and yet a further six years before these schemes were completed, forming the Bridgend to Nantyffyllon, and the Tondu to Porthcawl lines. The opening of these, as broad gauge branches off the South Wales Railway, was on 10th August 1861, under the auspices of the Llynfi Valley Railway. In 1873, now as part of the Llynfi & Ogmore Railway, they were absorbed by the GWR. The 1870s saw the completion of the railway network centred on Bridgend. The Garw and upper Ogmore valleys were opened up as were eastward connections to the Ely valley and the main line at Llanharan. Later, in the 1890s the Port Talbot Railway arrived from the west at Maesteg, Blaengarw and Cefn Junction, but that story must wait until the next chapter.

Elsewhere in the vale the speed of railway development following the opening of the South Wales Railway was initially no faster than that around Bridgend. The first branch built, by the Ely Valley Railway, from Llantrisant northwards to Tonyrefail was not opened until 1860. Progressive extensions eventually led to Blaenclydach and Gilfach Goch, the former extension tapping

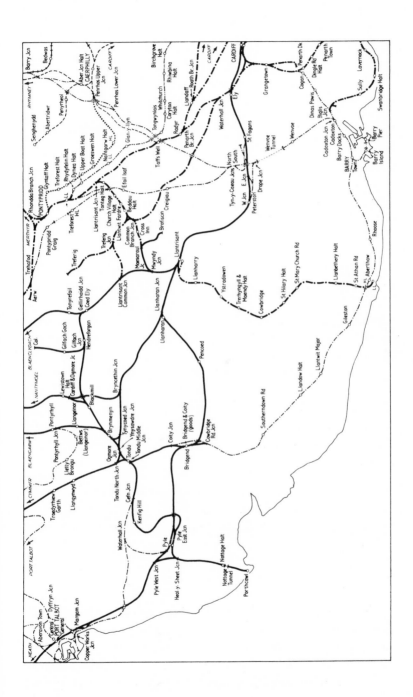

the same collieries as the Pwllyrhebog branch mentioned earlier. The extension to Blaenclydach must have seemed the ultimate justification to the Taff Vale Railway for its activities in this area during the 1860s. Initially the Taff Vale Railway became worried by the Ely Valley Railway in 1860, when it proposed to build its own standard gauge line to Cardiff. In fact this proposal frightened the GWR more than the TVR, for it immediately leased the line to forestall this move, and the consequent conversion of the rest of the system to the standard gauge. To counteract this threat the TVR sponsored a number of lines in the years from 1863 to 1886 in the area between Llantrisant and Treforest, the last of which ironically connected the Ely Valley line to the TVR at Radyr on the outskirts of Cardiff. Working these lines was not without its problems, since the SWR and Ely Valley lines were broad gauge. To give access to Llantrisant the GWR laid a third rail from Brofiskin, but not until twelve months after the TVR had opened its branch from Treforest in December 1863. Further expansion occurred south of the main line, beginning in 1865 when the Cowbridge Railway opened its single line from Llantrisant. Nominally an independent company, it was leased to the TVR from 1876. This again resulted in a peculiar working situation for the TVR, since from this date until the grouping it could only reach this outpost of its empire by running over GWR metals from Brofiskin and then reversing at Llantrisant. No further extension of this branch would have taken place had it not been for the Barry Railway. The TVR rightly recognised the Barry's threat at an early stage. In 1892 as one of a series of countermeasures it completed the extension of the Cowbridge branch to a small harbour at Aberthaw in the hope, one presumes, of developing it as an alternative outlet to Barry. Like the rest of its battles with the Barry Company, the TVR was doomed to failure yet again. Aberthaw harbour never developed; in fact it is doubtful if it could ever have been developed. Neither was the Barry Railway (thinly disguised as the Vale of Glamorgan Railway) forestalled in its westward thrust, for in 1899 the Barry to Bridgend line was opened, passing through Aberthaw.

After the burgeoning prosperity common to all the South

Wales railways up to World War I the lines in this area, in common with their neighbours, suffered the lingering death of the last half century. Of the lines around Llantrisant none now remain, and in the Bridgend area only the branch to Maesteg is still operational, but its future is far from assured.


## The Porthcawl Branch

The Dyffryn Llynfi & Porthcawl Railway, opened in 1828 from the Llynfi Valley, was a forerunner of the combined dock and railway company. Unfortunately, unlike its later rivals, it did not choose its dock site wisely. Built in the lee of a rocky promontory it was a tidal harbour on an exposed and treacherous coast. It had no river shelter, and was capable of only limited expansion as trade grew. These shortcomings were still not fully appreciated when the tramroad was taken over by the Llynfi Valley Railway on 22 July 1847. Not until about 1861 however was the conversion from tramroad to broad gauge steam railway completed, and even then a further four years elapsed before the first passenger service commenced on 1 August 1865, on what was soon to become the Llynfi & Ogmore Railway. Up to 1892, despite its drawbacks, the harbour did grow and achieved modest prosperity with coal exports balanced to some extent by pitwood and iron ore imports. Ten years later trade had almost ceased and in 1906 the dock was closed. Its drawbacks had become intolerable. Incapable of further expansion, its traffic from the Llynfi and Ogmore valley was tapped, at first indirectly, by the Barry Railway in the east, and with stunning swiftness after 1897, by the Port Talbot Railway in the west. Both companies, be it noted, were combined dock and railway undertakings, the very type of organisation which the old Duffryn Llynfi & Porthcawl had pioneered.

The fact that the railway did not die with the harbour was due to Porthcawl's remarkable and timely metamorphosis into a holiday resort. This development advanced sufficiently quickly during the opening years of this century for the GWR to build a new station 450yd south of the old station, on part of the old dock property. It was opened on 6 March 1916, to cater for the large numbers of visitors who even at this time flocked to Porthcawl. But it was built on the cheap; not for Porthcawl was there to be an imposing terminus. For just over 50 years the humble day-tripper, who made up the majority of the holiday traffic, had to put up with a building of timber framework and asbestos sheeting. No footbridge was provided, so those who did come to stay, and therefore had heavy luggage, had the daunting task of walking the length of the arrival platform before crossing behind the buffer stops and walking back the same way to the ticket office. Day trippers were more fortunate. For them a special gate was opened at the end of the arrival platform.

The branch started at Tondu and although easily graded south of the GWR main line at Pyle, it was extremely tortuous, a legacy of its tramway ancestry. The branch was sufficiently notorious in this respect that from 1906 to 1952, with a short gap around 1930, the Great Western and its successor kept at least one, and usually two, of the small 44xx class 2–6–2Ts stationed at Tondu to work the line. (These were the smallest of the Churchward standard 2–6–2Ts, with driving wheels of only 4ft 1½in diameter.) The peculiarities of working this branch were further recognised by the shed staff at Tondu. From about 1925 when two 44xxs were there, they would send out 4404 and 4408 the regular locomotives for over 25 years, one facing chimney to Porthcawl, and the other facing bunker to Porthcawl. On their return to Tondu about midday each would be reversed. This odd method of working was to even out flange wear, and was necessary even on these small locomotives.

Other locomotives were not precluded, particularly on the fast morning and evening businessmen's trains to Cardiff and Newport. In the 1920s these were regular Bulldog class 4–4–0 turns. On their withdrawal, a variety of large standard 2–6–2Ts worked the service. For many years 31xx class 3100 was a regular performer. The largest allowed were the 43xx class 2–6–0s. These were usually to be found on the summer excursion traffic which at one time was extremely heavy.

It was on such an excursion that I made my last steam-hauled journey on British Rail in August 1962 behind 7301. Twisting

away to the south from Pyle, for once the clear crisp Churchward exhaust beat was drowned by the continuous squeal of
wheel flanges from both locomotive and stock as we veered
sharply left, then right and finally left again. Once having
passed Cornelly Quarry and ducking beneath the Porthcawl to
Cornelly road, the curves eased over the flat ground running
towards Nottage and the outskirts of Porthcawl. Here with a
twist, a lurch and a whistle we passed Nottage Halt and dived
through Nottage tunnel, all of 63yd in length, before emerging
alongside the Porthcawl–Cornelly road. The mogul was now
eased to run past the old station and over the level crossing, to
halt at the terminus beside the long-closed inner harbour.

Rather oddly for a branch line terminus no shed or turntable was supplied, turn-round when necessary for tender locomotives being by running around a triangle of lines made up
partly of the old dock network. All trace of the terminus has now
disappeared. Whilst the railway may have gone, a relic of the old
tramway remains near the nearby breakwater. The tramway
once continued onto it, and some years ago a small section of
track was discovered there, and has been preserved *in situ.*

One and three-quarter miles west of Cefn Junction on the line
to Port Talbot was Waterhall Junction, and from here a second
single line once ran southwards to Pyle, but making an eastward-
facing connection. Originally part of the Cefn and Pyle Railway,
built to serve local collieries, it was bought by the Port Talbot
Railway and opened as one of its branches in 1898. Since its
closure it has vanished without a single trace, a rare event even
for a forgotten railway. Developments near Pyle station have
buried its southern end beneath the premises of a market garden
firm and a supermarket. Road improvements have completely
obliterated a level-crossing that once existed at SS 828825,
whilst north of this point a council estate has completely swal-
lowed it up. This little mineral branch, once a busy link to the
east for the Port Talbot Railway has just ceased to exist.

## Connections to the east

The complex of lines to the east of Tondu, which ultimately
resulted in two possible east-west alternative routes to the Great

Western main line, was the result of two classical forces in Victorian railway life. These were a clash of business interests and the desire to break an existing monopoly. The interests were those of the proprietors of the Llynfi Valley Railway and the Tondu Ironworks, the monopoly to be broken was that of the South Wales Railway. A common factor linked these two forces, and shaped the course of ultimate events. This was the personality of James Brogden, a partner in the Tondu Ironworks. Angered by the fact that the works was denied a connection to the LVR, and being dissatisfied with the arbitration damages awarded as a result, he determined that his company be independent of the LVR and its Porthcawl outlet. However, he later modified this latter objective. The outcome was his promotion with others of the Ogmore Valley and Ely Valley Extension Railways, both of which were started in 1863. The OVR was a standard gauge line (the LVR was broad gauge) running from collieries at Nantymoel to Tondu and then over a specially-laid third rail to Porthcawl. The Ely Valley Extension Railway, on the other hand, was a broad gauge line worked by the GWR from Gilfach Goch to Gellirhiad, where it joined the Ely Valley Railway. Both lines were completed in 1865.

Thoroughly frightened by the prospect of loss of traffic to the east despite the fact that the two new railways were over three miles apart and of differing gauges, the Board of the LVR made its peace with Brogden. Mergers then took place in 1865 and 1866 of all three concerns to form the Llynfi & Ogmore Railway, which became a narrow gauge line (except the Ely Valley Extension) in 1868. Within a few years, expansion of traffic necessitated a better eastward outlet, Bridgend now being of little use because of the break of gauge. To overcome this obstacle, and to deprive the GWR (as successor to the SWR) of its monopoly of eastbound traffic the L&O proposed a number of lines in that direction. These included a most unlikely proposal for a link with the Rhymney Railway. Events now quickly overtook the L&O, for the GWR at last realised the traffic potential of the South Wales valleys. As a result it replaced the broad gauge in 1872, which to some extent made the L&O schemes superfluous, and in the following year made a takeover bid that the L&O could not refuse, guaranteeing 6% return on ordinary shares. Thus the lines once projected in competition to the GWR were now completed in 1876 and 1877 by that company and ran from Black Mill to Hendreforgan, and from the Nantymoel branch at Cardiff & Ogmore Junction to Llanharan. This latter line was later linked via the Bryncethin Junction to Tynycoed Junction spur to the Llynfi Valley line.

The northernmost of these two single-line branches, to Gilfach Goch, provided a useful western outlet for the upper Ogmore valley, although the line was actually engineered to give an eastern outlet to the Ely Valley Railway. Logically, any passenger service should have been worked from Llantrisant, but this was not the case. Until its withdrawal in 1930 the passenger service was always worked from Tondu via Black Mill and Hendreforgan, where reversal took place for the final $1\frac{1}{4}$-mile dash to Gilfach Goch. Today it is difficult to appreciate the importance Gilfach Goch station once had in the affairs of the local community. It was the only reliable contact with the outside world, since in general the roads at the turn of the century were indifferent affairs at best. All the necessities of life were brought to it for the same reason. For decades its goods shed hummed with the activities associated with the trade of the town. Once a year its short platform, adorned with an unprepossessing wooden shelter and overlooked from its southern end by the mandatory signalbox, played host to the local children excitedly embarking on their annual outing to Porthcawl. Saturdays would see shoppers waiting for the 9.58am to Bridgend, for their weekly trip to Bridgend Market. Certainly such scenes were not unique to Gilfach Goch; in fact they would have been typical of nearly every station in a mining valley.

The second line, to Llanharan, was destined to become of great use to the GWR, since with the later connection from Margam Junction to Tondu it formed the eastern section of a diversion route for slow-moving mineral traffic, and for passenger traffic when engineering work was undertaken on the main line in the Bridgend area. As a 'red' route, only the King and 47xx classes were excluded. It was stiffly graded though, the climb out of Tondu towards Llanharan being particularly severe for some

three miles. As a result the maximum unassisted eastbound load
for a Castle was limited to 326 tons (394 tons westward) compared with 427 tons for main line workings between Cardiff and
Swansea. Through traffic on this little-known diversionary route
ceased when the section between Wern Tarw and Llanharan
closed in December 1962, whilst in the last few years the
continuing colliery closures have seen the demise of lines in both
the Ogmore and Garw valleys. These branches, to Nantymoel
and Blaengarw, have now joined their neighbours in the
lengthening catalogue of forgotten railways in South Wales, and
a brief description of them will be found in the Postscript.

## Great Western to the Rhondda

The Ely Valley Railway provided the GWR with its only connection to the Rhondda valley, or more accurately one of its off-
shoots, prior to 1923. Its final extension to Blaenclydach tapped
the Clydach Vale 11 years before the TVR arrived via an
extension from the head of its famous Pwllyrhebog incline, and
remained as its only exit for 16 years after the incline's closure.
Opened as a mineral line, a passenger service was provided from
1901, the accommodation for which gave Tonyrefail and
Penygraig the most handsome stations of any valley line. They
were pure GWR of the period. Long platforms (the branch was
double-tracked) were graced by single-storey combined ticket
office, waiting room, porters' room etc, with the provision of a
large awning which with its rooflike outline tended to over-
shadow the building, although it was greatly appreciated for its
ample protection in wet weather. Alas, such generous facilities
could not halt the decline in passenger traffic in post-war years,
and the service was withdrawn in 1958, some years before the
general closures in the area.

## The Taff Vale's rural outpost

The final result of the Taff Vale Railway's not too successful
efforts to fend off rivals along its western flank was to give
Glamorgan its only country branch. Running from Llantrisant

to Aberthaw through open rolling countryside, it had all the hallmarks of a rural branch, including the inevitable over-provision of facilities. A little under 12 miles in length and single-tracked, it boasted ten stations or halts, the former being spacious and equipped for all types of traffic. Cowbridge was the focal point of the branch and at the turn of the century was served, on Monday to Friday, by nine trains from Llantrisant, and nine return. Today, Cowbridge is $5\frac{1}{2}$ miles from the nearest railway, and $7\frac{3}{4}$ miles from the nearest station (Bridgend).

The Cowbridge Railway, incorporated in 1862, was built to connect Cowbridge with the South Wales Railway at Llantrisant. That it did so on the standard gauge is interesting, and says much either for the farsightedness of the Cowbridge Railway proprietors, or their relationship with the South Wales Railway. These had always been somewhat strained since the *volte-face* of the inhabitants of Cowbridge following the completion of the SWR. It had been Brunel's original intention to pass near the town, but local objections precluded this course, and the SWR never came closer than $5\frac{1}{2}$ miles. It also says much about what the SWR thought of this little local railway. Truly independent, the company at first ran its own services. Three locomotives were hired, from of all places Boulton's Siding, and included two of LNWR origin. The task soon became too much, and the Taff Vale Railway, seeking to consolidate its hold west of the Taff river leased the Cowbridge Railway from 1876.

There things would probably have rested had it not been for that thorn in the side of the TVR—the Barry Railway. For many years its docks and connecting rail system dealt a severe blow to the trade of the TVR, and its voracious appetite for expansion worried the latter immensely. It therefore had to respond to the Barry's proposed westward thrust via the Vale of Glamorgan Railway. This company had been cleverly taken over from the original proprietors, with coal interests in the Llynfi and Garw valleys. The route proposed ran close to the only potential harbour site left along the South Wales coast at this time—Aberthaw. The Taff Vale response was to back the supposedly independent Cowbridge & Aberthaw Railway in an effort to block the Barry. Yet again it was outflanked and outmanoeuvred, for Parliament sanctioned the Vale of Glamorgan and Cowbridge & Aberthaw Railways simultaneously in 1889. The line from Cowbridge was completed in 1892 and leased to the Taff Vale in 1895. In the event, the Barry never proposed any expansion in the Aberthaw area. Thus the TVR was left with a single-line branch, well built and expensively equipped, since it was to have competed with a powerful rival. It ran to a declining tidal harbour whose principal trade was shipping burnt lime from kilns on the foreshore to Bridgwater, for agricultural use in Somerset and Devon.

The branch's pleasantly proportioned red brick stations, with contrasting window and door surrounds of an attractive yellow brick, were served by the Taff Vale's distinctive railmotors. These were introduced from 1904, and offered both 1st and 3rd class accommodation. Among others of their breed they could be easily distinguished by the 'smokebox door' at the side of the power unit. After their demise, auto-train working became the rule under both TVR and GWR control. Shortly after World War II GWR diesel railcars worked the section from Llantrisant to Cowbridge, for by this time the line southwards to Aberthaw had long since joined the ghosts of railways past. As on many a rural branch the mainstay of motive power during the final years was the 14xx class 0–4–2T. 1471 was a regular performer for over 13 years up to the branch's closure in 1951.

The Cowbridge to Aberthaw section closed finally in 1931. Yet surprisingly it is only on this section that one can find reminders of the line's past. The station buildings of St Mary Church Road and St Athan Road still stand to this day. Both are now privately-owned, and the former is in excellent external condition on a site still recognisable as a station. 56 years after closure, and 95 after construction, they are all that is left of the TVR dash to the sea.

## Taff Vale lines around Llantrisant

Of the single-line network built by the TVR north of the GWR main line, only the Treforest to Llantrisant branch offered a passenger service. Never as prosperous as the remainder of the

TVR system, only a few collieries near Llantwit Fardre
sustained a substantial volume of traffic. In fact the last surviving
section of this network served the last remaining colliery (Cwm
Llantwit), and a limestone quarry, as sidings from Llantrisant.

The direct Taff Vale link (between Llantrisant Common
Junction and Common Branch Junction) from the Ely valley to
their Penarth Dock branch at Waterhall Junction closed shortly
after the grouping. The hopes that the Taff Vale entertained
about this line's usefulness can still be seen in the size of the
abandoned earthworks and the abutments of the overbridge on
the A4119 at ST 031846. The Treferig branch which led off
northwards from this link, about 200yd east of the site of the
Royal Mint, closed at the same time. This line is now only
recalled by those who remember its usefulness as a footpath in
a lonely yet beautiful valley with no adequate road. Today that
use is hard to visualise. Dense woods have now grown over much
of its length in the 63 years since its closure, and the stream
alongside which it ran, has ensured that much now remaining
resembles a swamp.

The Waterhall Junction to Common Branch Junction line,
sustained for many years by one morning trip to Creigiau quarry
and an afternoon working to Cwm Colliery on the Llantrisant to
Treforest line, eventually succumbed in 1964. The principal
outlet for the limestone from Creigiau was the East Moors steelworks in Cardiff, which incidentally was supplied with high-
grade iron-ore from the Llanharry mine at the northern end of
the Cowbridge branch, until its closure in 1975. Now the steelworks too has closed, and has joined the lines that served it in
half-forgotten memory.

Only three excursion trains ever gave the line any passenger
traffic. One was an official TVR works outing, the second (just
prior to World War I) was a Sunday school trip, whilst the third
was a railtour in 1952. The line was known officially as the
'Llantrisant No 1 railway', and unofficially as the 'old rusty
line', eloquent testimony to its intensive use! This lack of traffic
though was put to good account by the TVR in 1903/4. In
that period the newly-constructed steam railmotors were extensively tested on the branch before being put into service.

# CHAPTER 8

# Port Talbot to Swansea

The railways that served the hinterland behind Port Talbot at first sight present a puzzle. Geographically the only outlet is via the Afan valley running in a north-westerly direction from the coast, and the three principal local railways can be found in various parts of the main valley or its major tributaries. Now comes the puzzle. The first line opened between 1861 and 1863 was the broad gauge South Wales Mineral Railway. It ran from Glyncorrwg then down the Afan valley for a few miles, then instead of continuing to Port Talbot, turned through a tunnel into the Pelena valley and thence over the hills to Briton Ferry. The second railway was the Rhondda & Swansea Bay Railway. Having tunnelled from the Rhondda valley in 1890 it ran all the way down the Afan valley, but ignored Port Talbot, except for a short spur to the dock, and turned instead along the coast to Swansea. Finally came the Port Talbot Railway, in 1897 and 1898. This company rebuilt and enlarged the inadequate harbour, and then took itself off to the Garw valley via the steep and narrow vale of Duffryn. Later it repented and did use the Afan valley for a connection to the SWMR at Tonmawr.

Easily understandable business interests dictated the routes of the R&SB and PTR. The former was backed by financial interests which wished to bring to the docks at Swansea some of the prodigious quantities of coal being mined in the Rhondda. The latter company was influenced by businessmen with colliery interests in the Llynfi and Garw valleys, who were frustrated by the inadequacies of the tidal harbour at Porthcawl. The route selected for the SWMR has little to offer in the way of a logical explanation, except that it was perhaps the shortest route to Briton Ferry, the nearest useful harbour to Glyncorrwg that

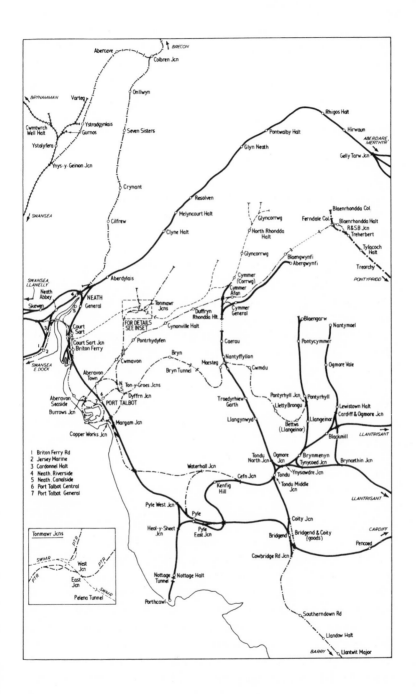

existed when the route was surveyed by Brunel in the 1850s.

From its opening in 1897, the GWR was always kindly disposed to the PTR. It too was frustrated by Porthcawl's inadequate harbour which it had acquired with the Llynfi & Ogmore Railway in 1873, and frightened by the possibility of losing traffic over the Vale of Glamorgan line to the Barry Railway, it therefore looked upon the facilities of the new harbour at Port Talbot as the relief to these frustrations. Similarly the R&SB, after an initial period of antagonism due to its parallel and competitive route between Port Talbot and Swansea, was also courted by the GWR. Here the reasons were slightly different. In addition to the obvious advantages to be gained from access to the Rhondda traffic, the GWR was planning its avoiding line in the Swansea area, and the R&SB's crossing of the river Neath was to be a link in this network.

By giving suitable financial guarantees the GWR achieved its objectives, obtaining running powers over the complete network of all three railways. 1 January 1906 saw agreement with the R&SB, while exactly two years later similar agreements were signed with the PTR and SWMR. The latter was by now dependent on the PTR for working its traffic out of the valley. From now until the Grouping all three became progressively more closely associated with the GWR. Even though they maintained their own boards of directors, locomotives, rolling stock and so on, they were an integral part of the Great Western Railway in all but name.

### To Glyncorrwg the hard way

It was unusual in South Wales to find a railway worked by a colliery company that it served. As a result, the fortunes of the South Wales Mineral Railway mirrored those of the Glyncorrwg Coal Company, and when it failed the railway too went bankrupt. Only the efforts of the SWMR secretary, T. J. Woods, who was appointed receiver, kept the railway going from 1878 to 1880. In the latter year the reformed coal company commenced trading again, and took on once more the working of the SWMR. The reasons why it came to be in this position were many, and date back to its inception in the early 1850s. The SWMR was conceived as a line to link the then developing Glyncorrwg mining area to the South Wales Railway at Briton Ferry, and the nearby harbour. Brunel was the engineer, though he never saw it completed. He chose a most difficult route, and a most inappropriate gauge for a mineral line, his broad gauge of 7ft 0¼in. The directors, London businessmen, had financial interests in the coal company. These interests blinded them to the fact that a single source of income to the railway could give rise to financial instability, and possibly restrict future investment capital. Thus on 15 August 1853 the South Wales Mineral Railway was incorporated, with all these inherent faults. Bankruptcy at some future date was inevitable.

In fairness to Brunel one must concede that he surveyed the shortest route between Glyncorrwg and Briton Ferry. That it included a rope-worked incline, a 1109yd tunnel, followed by a 2¾-mile hillside shelf to the entrance of Glyncorrwg, appears inexcusable in retrospect. With gradients as steep as 1 in 22 the line ran down Glyngorrwg and turned westward into the Afan valley, along the southern flank of Mynydd Nant-y-bar. Near Gyfylchi it turned sharply north-west through the tunnel into the adjacent Pelena valley. From the mouth of Glyncorrwg to this point the gradients were much easier, falling at between 1 in 72 and 1 in 104. Beyond the tunnel to the top of the incline Brunel maintained negligible gradients by clever contour hugging. Thus this broad gauge line came to the heights above Briton Ferry, at a level of some 450ft above the town. From here the 1½ mile Ynys-y-Maerdy incline connected it with what was then the South Wales Railway.

Not surprisingly the line was expensive to build, and construction of the tunnel caused considerable delay. In 1855 the SWMR was leased to the Glyncorrwg Coal Company for 30 years. However, a further six years were to elapse before the line was completed as far as the west end of the tunnel, and another two before the line opened to Glyncorrwg on 10 March 1863. Notwithstanding these delays, and the obvious handicaps of the line its directors, in true Victorian railway fashion, were not content to let things rest there. The following year they applied, and obtained consent, for a branch continuing up the Afan valley to Blaenavon. In the event this branch was never constructed.

The railway, which was worked by the coal company from 1870, had not sufficiently recovered from its protracted construction phase when the GWR converted its South Wales lines to the standard gauge in 1872. From this extra financial burden, coupled with a slump in the mining industry, both railway and coal company never recovered. The colliery went bankrupt in 1878, dragging the SWMR down with it. The railway remained in the hands of the receiver for 29 years until taken-over by the GWR from 1 January 1908, as part of its expansion in this area. In actual fact the line was run by the Port Talbot Railway from this date, taking over the running from the Glyncorrwg Colliery Company. This latter was the successor of the old Glyncorrwg Coal Company, and had worked the line from 1880.

The PTR's interest in the SWMR dated from 1898. On 14 November of that year it completed its line from Tonygroes Junction in Port Talbot to Tonmawr in the Pelena valley, and simultaneously opened two branches to tap two new collieries nearby. The SWMR could not be extended for this traffic, nor for that matter could it cope properly with the increasing output from Glyncorrwg, due to the bottleneck of the incline. The PTR connection at Tonmawr therefore offered welcome relief, and a close relationship grew up between the two companies. This culminated in the abandonment of the incline in 1910.

Following the 1908 agreement a measure of modest prosperity was achieved for the first time in the railway's history. So much so that in 1918 (of all years) a public passenger service commenced between Cymmer and Glyncorrwg, over the GWR line from Nantyffyllon in the Llynfi valley, which had been opened in 1878. Much later this connection provided the only exit from Glyncorrwg after the closure of Tonmawr tunnel in 1947 following a landslide. This service ceased in 1930, although unadvertised miners' trains were not finally withdrawn until 2 November 1964.

Some of the public passenger workings ran as mixed trains, wagons being attached behind what was usually a single coach. From a contemporary photograph it appears that the stock was

*Plates 17 and 18.* More local trains. *Above*: Former-GWR 0-6-2T No 6605 at Hirwaun in 1962, having just arrived with a Neath–Pontypool Road train. *Below*: 'The St Fagans Pullman' – ex-GWR 0-6-0PT No 6438 on a Pontypridd–Cardiff auto-train in 1959, between Tynycaeau Junction and St Fagans. The nearer bridge carried the Barry Railway main line across the branch; the further one is a farm crossing. (*Glyn Davies, R.O. Tuck*)

*Plates 19 and 20.* Station contrasts. *Above*: The simple platform at Llwydcoed on the GWR Aberdare–Merthyr line. *Below*: Quakers Yard. GWR 0-6-2T No 5680 stands in the former Taff Vale Railway Low Level station, while in the background can be seen the former GWR High Level station, on the Pontypool Road–Neath line. Note the long connecting footbridge. (*Glyn Davies, Brian Moone*)

of GWR origin (Dean clerestory), but whether bought, loaned or hired by the SWMR is not certain. This stock in fact survived at least until the mid-1950s on the workmen's trains. The single platform stations at Glyncorrwg and Cymmer Corrwg were spartan to say the least. Cymmer Corrwg consisted of one single-storey brick building, with no awning for protection against the weather, and a gentlemen's toilet at the north end of the single platform. It must be admitted that this says a lot for someone's ideas of priorities when travelling! However the ultimate in minimum facilities was reached at North Rhondda Halt, which served the colliery at the head of the valley. Here existed a mere collection of timbers built up to the appropriate height, not even graced by a nameboard.

### To Glyncorrwg the easy way

The second railway to enter the Afan valley was the GWR. In 1878 its extension of the Llynfi & Ogmore Railway, which it had taken over in 1873, was completed from Nantyffyllon through the Caerau tunnel to Cymmer. Mineral extensions to Abergwynfi at the head of the Afan valley, and to the SWMR south of Glyncorrwg via a high single-span girder bridge, were opened at the same time. Now traffic from the Corrwg valley had an effi-cient exit. Alas, it came too late to save the Glyncorrwg com-pany, whose bankruptcy was imminent.

Luckily the Great Western branch had other sources of traffic, notably the Avon colliery at Abergwynfi, sunk in 1877 by a company which numbered amongst its early directors Sir Daniel Gooch. It was bought by the GWR in 1905, and worked by it until 1912 when it was sold in a very run-down condition. Strangely, the position here was the exact reverse to that of the SWMR and the Glyncorrwg Coal Company. There the colliery ran the railway, to the latter's detriment—here the railway ran the colliery, also to the latter's detriment, an example perhaps proving that a cobbler should stick to his last.

This quiet backwater of the GWR gave the small isolated village of Cymmer its first station in 1880. Ultimately, no less than three were to serve this community, which never numbered above a few hundred souls. The passenger service was extended to the equally small and isolated village of Abergwynfi in 1886. The story of the branch's later years is told in the following section.

### Swansea to the Rhondda

Born out of the frustrations caused by the inadequacies of the Taff Vale Railway, the only line to use the Afan valley for its full length did so as an afterthought, and almost ignored Port Talbot completely. Its route down that valley, thence along the coast to Briton Ferry where it crossed the Neath river and ran to the docks at Swansea, appears straightforward and logical. Apart from the 1 mile 1683yd Rhondda tunnel there appears little in the way of impediment that could have delayed its construction. In fact, the Rhondda & Swansea Bay Railway obtained its Act of Incorporation on 10 August 1882, but did not reach its terminus at Swansea (Riverside) until 7 May 1899, a little under 17 years for a railway only 24 miles 31 chains long.

In 1880 two schemes had been promoted to link the Rhondda Fawr with Swansea. The first was for a railway from Swansea to the SWMR at Briton Ferry, thence via a tunnel from Glyncorrwg to the head of the Rhondda valley. The second, which was that of the R&SBR, was for a line from Swansea to Baglan (south-east of Briton Ferry). From there a tunnel was proposed to near Pontrhydyfen. The valley was then to be followed to a point where a second tunnel could be bored to reach the Rhondda. From Pontrhydyfen a branch was to run down the Afan to Aberavon and Port Talbot dock. It is interesting to note, even at this later date, how the R&SBR promoters, like those of the SWMR nearly 30 years before, were obsessed by the concept that a railway should be built by the shortest route, irrespective of geographical considerations.

The start of the R&SBR's 17-year struggle stemmed from its Act of Incorporation. Because of objections from local shipping interests to the proposed river bridge below the town of Neath, the line was sanctioned from Treherbert only as far as Briton Ferry. Denied entry into Swansea, from which much of the railway's backing originated, the R&SBR came to an agreement with the GWR to work its traffic from Port Talbot to Swansea. The R&SBR was thus obliged to use the Afan valley below Pontyhydyfen. The advantages of the Port Talbot route were soon evident, and the company quickly abandoned all thought of the Baglan tunnel. However, not for the first time did a small railway find agreement with the GWR irksome, and to the advantage of that company. It therefore resolved to renew attempts to gain independent access to Swansea, and in 1892 sought to revive powers obtained in 1886 to build from Aberavon to Briton Ferry, thence across the Neath river to the original objective. Not content to let things rest there, it obtained access to Briton Ferry dock, and to its own station in Neath (Canal Side). All of this was parallel to the GWR and bitterly opposed by that company. Completion of these lines took seven years, the line at Briton Ferry passing twice beneath the GWR main line. The cost was immense, and for many years was reflected in the dividends, or more correctly, lack of them. Prosperity did come however, for the South Wales coalfield was approaching its peak, enabling the R&SBR to obtain very advantageous terms when the running of the line was taken-over by the GWR in 1906.

To travel to Swansea over the R&SBR route was always different, even though the journey included ingredients found on most South Wales valley lines. The starts on the rising gradients at Treherbert and Blaenrhondda were guaranteed to be exhilarating; the presence of a 56xx class 0–6–2T would ensure that. Beyond Blaenrhondda lay the single-line bore of the Rhondda tunnel, up to which one climbed at a steady 1 in 55. Here nature almost defeated the engineer in his attempts to provide ventilation. Mynydd Blaengwynfi rises almost vertically above the Rhondda valley entrance, eventually towering some 900ft above the tunnel roof. As a result only one shaft was possible, close to the end. This, combined with the restricted dimensions of the bore made working conditions well nigh intolerable on the footplate or in the guard's van. Leaving the tunnel on a right-hand curve the GWR line to Abergwynfi swung into view, and ran parallel to the Rhondda line beyond Blaengwynfi station. Both independent lines paralleled each other through every twist of the narrow upper Afan valley until Cymmer was reached. The surprise of this stretch occurred a little above Cymmer. Having run through a bleak treeless section, one crossed the river rounded a sharp bend and plunged into a narrow wooded ravine, before entering a short tunnel. Such an accompaniment to a rail journey in the valleys was a rarity, although on the northern slopes of the valley some way beyond Cymmer there were striking views of the Michaelston Forest. It was through this forest that the SWMR ran to Glyncorrwg.

Once below Pontrhydyfen, at which place the PTR viaduct never failed to impress, one could be excused for thinking that the line held no more surprises as it ran through an area desolated by 19th century industry. This final surprise came south of Port Talbot (Aberavon) station where the R&SBR line crossed the GWR main line on the level. Crossing here at a stately 15mph was an experience not to be forgotten. The final part of the journey was through Aberavon (Sea Side), near the popular Aberavon Sands, and then across a flat windswept landscape, with sand dunes for company, to Briton Ferry where the main line was joined for the remainder of the journey to Swansea. Such was a journey some 34 years ago, and the changes beyond Briton Ferry will be noted. These were introduced by the GWR between 1906 and 1947, and although they were gradual they completely destroyed the individuality of the line from here on.

Following the 1906 takeover the passenger services were brought into line with those of the larger company, which even went so far as to provide three modern passenger locomotives for this traffic. It may perhaps come as a surprise to realise that these locomotives were 45xx 2–6–2Ts, the doyens of the country branch line, sent new from Wolverhampton where they had been amongst the last locomotives built there. 4504–6, orginally GWR 2165–2167, were numbered 31–3 in R&SBR stock and were returned to the GWR between 1912 and 1914, (4504/5 via the PTR). Here they continued their lives in the manner for which the class is best remembered. They ended their service in the mid-1950s at Truro, St Blazey and Neyland respectively.

1915 saw the R&SBR linked to the Swansea District Line,

one of the reasons behind the 1906 amalgamation, and 1936 saw the diversion of all R&SBR passenger traffic to Swansea (High Street) following the rebuilding of Briton Ferry station a year earlier. It is a pleasure to record, though, that these lines west of Briton Ferry still remain open. Although much modified they still form a part of the complex rail approach to Swansea Docks. All R&SBR tracks to the east of Briton Ferry have now disappeared, and until one is north of Port Talbot not even the trackbed can be found, such has been the extent of development in this area following closure in the 1960s. Redevelopment has also destroyed all trace at Blaengwynfi, where desperate attempts are being made to attract industry to this isolated community.

## Port Talbot's own railway

In the closing years of the last century the restrictions imposed on coal export traffic by the inadequacies of the harbour at Porthcawl became intolerable to the mine owners of the Lynfi, Garw and Ogmore valleys. The Great Western was unable (or unwilling) to improve the harbour, since while perhaps it could have been enlarged its seaward approach was treacherous. The first attempt to get an alternative outlet found the coal owners proposing a connection to the new harbour at Barry to satisfy their needs. Although proposed by the Llynfi valley interests etc, the line, incorporated in 1889 as the Vale of Glamorgan Railway, was built and ultimately worked by the Barry Railway. This arrangement would have suited everybody, had the line not taken eleven years to complete. Long before completion, however, the mine owners viewing the slow rate of construction of the V of GR sought another alternative, and turned their eyes westward to Port Talbot.

The company formed was, like the Barry Railway, a combined railway and dock company. It was incorporated on 31 July 1894 to enlarge the existing tidal harbour at Port Talbot, dating from around 1837, and to build a railway via Maesteg to the Garw·valley at Pontyrhyll, with running powers over the GWR to the head of the valley. By separate Acts in 1896 two branches were sanctioned. The first ran up the Afan and Pelena valleys to join the SWMR at Tonmawr. The second, under the title of the Ogmore Valley Extension Railway ran to Cefn Junction on the Tondu to Porthcawl branch of the GWR. Of the old PTR system only this branch survives today, much modified at its western end. January 1898 saw the opening of the main line to Pontyrhyll and both branches were completed by the end of that year, two years ahead of the Vale of Glamorgan Railway.

The PTR and a proposed westward extension of the Vale of Glamorgan line by the Barry Railway posed two threats to the monopoly of traffic in the area between Bridgend and Swansea held by the GWR. It sought to retain its monopoly in the Bridgend area by assisting the infant PTR, and working the traffic over the Ogmore Valley Extension Railway from its opening. Thereafter it continued to remain on the friendliest of terms; hence when it proposed a running powers agreement in 1908, similar to that in operation with the R&SBR, it met with no opposition from the PTR shareholders. Following these two agreements the Barry Railway abandoned its schemes for a westward expansion, removing the second threat to the GWR monopoly.

The main line ran from Port Talbot (Central) station which stood on the opposite side of the road from the main line station. Its ruins can still be found next to a cinema. From this terminus it swung east and then north into the Duffryn valley to Maesteg and Pontyrhyll. Even today, beyond the entrance to this valley, where a housing estate has been built on the site of the railway's main depot, Duffryn Yard, it is lonely and isolated. As a result this section as far as Cwm Cerwin tunnel (1012yd) which is on a continuously rising gradient of 1 in 40 for about $3\frac{1}{2}$ miles, is better preserved than any other comparable length in South Wales. A unique feature of the Port Talbot Railway was that the majority of its bridges were of red brick, and every one built on this stretch is still intact.

Beyond the tunnel, which still proudly bears the inscription 'PTR 1897' above its red brick eastern entrance, the line swung in a large S-bend around Maesteg. Strangely, it avoided any direct contact with the GWR. It served collieries on the east side

of the Llynfi valley as far as Lletty Brongu, then curved eastwards to Pontyrhyll and the GWR branch up the Garw valley.
The outstanding feature of this section is the viaduct near
Llangynwyd. 114yd long, and 73ft high, it has seven arches of
40ft span and one of 20ft span. It stands to this day in remote
isolation guarding, in red brick splendour, the entrance of a
small valley off that of the Llynfi.

The branch to Tonmawr is not without interest. The start at
Tonygroes Junction now lies in part beneath the M4 motorway,
but north of here it is still possible to trace the line up the eastern
side of the Afan valley. At Cwmavon it crossed the R&SBR on
the skew by way of a lattice girder bridge of two 68ft spans, and
once maintained interchange sidings here. The line this far from
Tonygroes was abandoned in 1954 when a new connection was
laid to the R&SBR line. Beyond, at Pontrhydyfen, and still intact,
stands the Port Talbot Railway's other viaduct. Slightly lower
at 70ft than that at Llangynwyd, it curves gracefully to lead the
line into the Pelena valley via ten arches of 40ft span. Like its
companion, it is built in red brick. For those sufficiently determined, a surprise awaits at Tonmawr. Here the PTR met the
SWMR and also threw off its own colliery branches. It was no
simple junction however. Its size, and one-time importance can
be judged from the extensive earthworks that remain here. It is
also interesting to note that the junction was not all at one level.
In fact it existed over three distinct levels.

A branch of the PTR ran southwards from Duffryn Junction,
crossed the main line by a 70ft single-span lattice girder bridge
built on the skew, and ran to the south side of the harbour.
Travelling westward along the main line one may be excused for
thinking that the red brick embankment and bridge remains seen
1¼ miles east of Port Talbot station, and apparently running into
the nearby steelworks are the original PTR structures. The
steelworks seen today was created by extensive additions and
updating of existing facilities shortly after World War II, and
the PTR dock branch via Copper Works Junction, impeded this
expansion. Thus in 1947 the crossing of the main line was moved
slightly eastwards and the branch southwards from here lifted
some 12 to 15ft for much of its length. Obviously considerable

realignment of dock and adjacent sidings took place at this time. However Copper Works Junction was reinstated in its original position, but about 12ft higher. For reasons now forgotten though, the GWR rebuilt this section of the branch in a style similar to that of the old railway company. The bridges, and the embankment near the main line are in fact constructed of reinforced concrete, cast *in situ*. The red brick is merely a facing that matched the remainder of the system. Although closed north of the resited Copper Works Junction, the short southern portion is used by the 1000-tonne ore trains that ply between Port Talbot and Llanwern steelworks.

Only the larger civil engineering structures remain today to remind one of this railway, so long a part of the GWR in all but name before the official amalgamation in 1922. This is a great pity, for with the destruction of every PTR building, signalbox etc, has been lost the evidence of the close similarity of these structures to their GWR counterparts. Early photographs show this similarity clearly; in fact at a cursory glance only the station names indicate that one is not looking at a GWR station. Even the style of painting was similar with a dark colour used below waist height, and a light colour above. Only a close examination reveals any feature that could distinguish them from GWR stations. Such an examination shows that the station names are actually etched in the glass of the station gas lamps, even though the overall design of these lamps appears typically Great Western.

Although its locomotive stock was influenced and in a few cases supplemented by the Barry Railway, due to the two locomotive superintendents being brothers, the influence of the GWR could also be found. Before the 1908 agreement, which saw standard GWR types used on the system, including two of the 45xx class on their way back to the GWR proper from the R&SBR lines, the PTR ordered a steam railmotor from R. & W. Hawthorn Leslie & Company Limited. This was similar to the larger GWR units in use at this time, even down to the encased power unit. The only major design departure was the use of a 6-coupled power unit as opposed to the more normal 4-coupled, as a concession to the continuous 1 in 40 ascent to Bryn.

# CHAPTER 9

# Swansea to Llanelly

Swansea was the only South Wales town to which three national railway companies had access. These were the GWR, LNWR and MR, each of which entered having leased or absorbed local companies. Had the GWR been a little more perceptive things would have been entirely different, but as related previously it never really woke up to the potential traffic in South Wales until late in the 19th century, by which time its rivals were firmly entrenched. Even then it only took on the Midland Railway seriously, firstly using the Swansea Canal which it had purchased in 1873, and from 1881 opening competing lines in the Swansea valley, the last of which was not opened until 1923.

Two of the oldest railways sanctioned by Parliament, the Carmarthenshire of 1802 and the Oystermouth of 1804 lay within this region of South Wales. The former has survived the years (transformed in 1875 to the Llanelly & Mynydd Mawr Railway) and remains as a branch from Llanelly to Cynheidre; the latter ceased operation (as the Mumbles Railway) in 1960. These pioneers were followed in 1828 by the Llanelly Dock & Railway Company, which over the years built lines from Llanelly to Llandilo (1839–1857), Llandilo to Carmarthen (1864), and Pontardulais to Swansea (1866). The inept management of this company was now used by the LNWR, which was seeking access to the South Wales coalfield via its line from Craven Arms which met the Vale of Towy Railway (leased to the Llanelly company) at Llandovery. Following a series of manoeuvres the Llanelly company was obliged to sell the Carmarthen, Swansea and Llanmorlais branches to the LNWR. Thus the latter completed its celebrated Central Wales line which today, although terminating at Llanelly, stubbornly refuses to die.

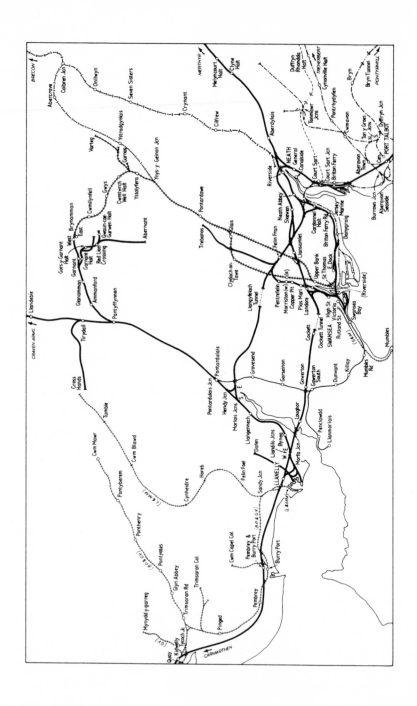

1850 saw the broad gauge South Wales Railway reach Swansea, and two years later, its extension through Llanelly, which crossed the Llanelly Railway twice on the level in a short distance. In 1863 the V of N, also broad gauge, entered Swansea along the coast from the east, both systems joining south of High Street station. Swansea's final entrant (the R&SBR) was to build along a course parallel to the V of N between 1894 and 1899.

The Midland Railway's entry came via the Swansea Vale Railway in 1874. This company's aim of reaching Swansea, described in Chapter 2, was completed by running powers over the Swansea Vale and Neath & Brecon Railways from Colbren to Ynisygeinon, whence a lease and later purchase of the Swansea Vale Railway gave it access to Swansea itself.

## The GWR in Swansea

Despite the loss of local passenger services and radically altered freight and shipping patterns, the GWR lines have only lost a relatively small mileage in and around Swansea compared with the total extinction of the once rival lines of the LNWR and Midland Railways.

The branch from Hafod Junction to Felin Fran was built in two sections, opening to Morriston in 1881 and Felin Fran in 1914. It was the Great Western's belated answer to the presence of the Midland, which had entered the Swansea valley seven years before the opening of the first section. Why the GWR delayed building for so long is a mystery.

Dropping steeply from Hafod Junction (SS 660952) high above the A4067 road, it ran for its entire length alongside and just to the east of this road until it climbed steeply eastwards across the Midland's line to gain the Swansea Avoiding Line at Felin Fran Junction (West). Its course can still be traced in parts, but the redevelopment under way in this area is rapidly encroaching on the trackbed. Only the derelict soot-stained stone station building at Morriston remains of the five stations that once existed on this line.

That the route ran parallel to a main road mattered little prior to World War I, for it was the only access for men and materials to the numerous smelters and refineries along its path. The recession dealt a cruel blow as elsewhere to these industries, and with the simultaneous development of bus transport, resulted in the demise of passenger services in 1965.

Further north the GWR made its last attempt to develop coal traffic in the Swansea valley. In 1911 it obtained powers to build northwards from Felin Fran to Clydach and Trebanos, thence up the upper Clydach valley to join the branch from Pantyffynnon to Gwaun-cae-Gurwen. Construction having reached Clydach in 1914 halted during the war. The branch was eventually completed to Trebanos in 1923, but the section northwards was never built. It is still in use as far as Clydach, serving a nickel refinery, the extension to Trebanos having closed in 1965. Few traces now remain of this short-lived extension, noteworthy as the Great Western's last attempt in developing coal traffic in South Wales.

Alongside the road between the South and East Docks, and along the northern side of the former, it is still possible to see short isolated lengths of what were once substantially-built stone viaducts. Except with the aid of a map it is difficult to visualise that these lengths were once joined in a high-level rail system linking Swansea's dock complex and providing direct access from the rail network serving the town. In this area there was for many years a complicated ground-level network complementing the high level, built and worked by the Swansea Harbour Trust. Much of the high-level, and all of the low-level lines have been removed in recent years to improve the local road network, leaving only a few lengths of isolated viaduct like pieces of a jigsaw puzzle.

The high-level system was constructed between 1852 and 1863 by the GWR, Swansea Harbour Trust, and the V of N, although in 1862 the SHT leased its section to the V of N. It ran from North Dock Junction (just north of High Street) to South Dock, where from 1866 it made connection with the LNWR west of Victoria station. At Wind Street Junction the V of N line from the East Dock joined, and until March 1873 was the terminus of the V of N passenger service. Although only goods lines from this date, passenger traffic made rare appearances when diversions were necessary. The first was for an extended period in 1899 following the collapse of Cockett tunnel on the GWR main line. The last was in December 1961 when an accident closed the former LNWR line near Gorseinon, and the passengers of the 6.30pm Swansea (Victoria) to York had the unusual experience of reversing about ¼-mile outside Victoria, before slowly wending their way above the lighted streets to gain the Western Region main line outside High Street.

### The North Western in Swansea

The railway from Pontardulais to Swansea and the single-line branch to Llanmorlais formed the southern section of the well-known LNWR Central Wales line, and is the only part to have suffered closure. (Swansea traffic now works via Llanelly, where a reversal is necessary to reach High Street). It has been told in Chapter 4 how the LNWR in its bid for access to the South Wales coalfield achieved its initial foothold on its eventual route to Merthyr by the tactic of cultivating a friendly relationship with a local company before leasing and subsequent absorption. A similar ploy between the years 1861–1868 was equally successful further west, resulting in the North Western gaining access via running powers over the Llanelly Railway's Pontardulais to Swansea branch (opened 1866) and, incidentally, the Llandilo to Carmarthen branch (see Chapter 10). Unlike the Merthyr, Tredegar & Abergavenny the Llanelly Railway immediately regretted its decision and fought the North Western all the way to the House of Lords in a bid to terminate its agreement. The surprising outcome was that both branches were formed into the Swansea & Carmarthen Railway in 1871, and worked from the outset by the LNWR. Two years later the Llanelly company capitulated, sold the S&C to the North Western and retired from the scene, leaving the Premier Line in sole ownership. Amongst all the railway battles of the last century, this perhaps had the most unexpected outcome.

The Swansea branch, some 12½ miles long, was a line of contrasts. It diverged at Pontardulais, whose distinctive feature was the footbridge that spanned all four platforms (two on the Llanelly line and two on the branch), and firstly ran through an industrial landscape of pit workings and steelworks. Beyond Dunvant (6½ miles), however, the scenery changed dramatically as the line descended via Killay through the attractive Clyne woods before bursting out on to the sea shore beyond Mumbles Road station. This stretch, along the very edge of Swansea Bay, commanding the most delightful views along the Gower coast, provided the operating authorities with one of their more unusual problems—keeping the sand off the tracks. At least a surefooted restart from Swansea Bay station, an exposed wooden structure, was always assured!

Just before Victoria station the line swung inland and connections to the high-level lines, Paxton Street shed, and the South Dock diverged to the right. The two platforms of Victoria station were once spanned by an all-over glass roof supported on iron columns, which was partially destroyed in an air raid. This damage was never repaired, a state of affairs which added greatly to Victoria's run-down appearance in later years. A possible reason for this neglect was that from 1948 the line passed to the Western Region of British Railways, which had no love for this ex-rival.

Paxton Street depot, or 87K Swansea (Victoria) as it was known in BR ownership, was of typical LNWR design with six straight roads, and was always a source of interest to South Wales enthusiasts. Whereas at Abergavenny the Coal Tanks or G2 0–8–0s were the mainstay, here it was possible to find a Black Five, an 8F or perhaps a Jubilee.

To the credit of the local council Victoria station and much of its surroundings have been completely and most imaginatively rebuilt. A leisure centre complex has risen on the station site and alongside, set into the embankment that once led to the high-level lines, has been built an outdoor theatre designed as a classical Greek amphitheatre in miniature. Behind, but linked to the complex, a dock warehouse has been converted into a Maritime and Industrial Museum.

At Gowerton South converged the lonely branch from Llanmorlais on the north Gower coast, and built originally to serve mineral interests in the area. The line ran along the edge of windswept saltmarsh for much of its way, through scenery reminiscent of the north Brittany coast west of Mont St Michel. It is remembered today for the cockle traffic that originated at Penclawdd, providing the staple traffic of the branch for many years until the advent of the motor lorry. Passenger services ceased in 1931, freight in 1957.

## The Midland in Swansea

The absorption and ultimate purchase of the Swansea Vale Railway by the Midland was merely a step along that company's path to gaining control of its own independent route to the industrial riches of South Wales (see also Chapter 2). The SVR was built as a private railway serving local industry in the Swansea valley. Its position was regularised by an Act of 1855, and by 1864 its single line had extended to Ynysgedwyn and on to Brynamman, where it made an end-on junction with the Llanelly Railway's branch from Pantyffynon.

Built as cheaply as possible by proprietors who totally underestimated the growth of traffic, it was by the early 1870s rundown and desperately in need of modernising. It was therefore easy prey for such a predator as the Midland, which softened any possible opposition by friendly overtures and the loan of locomotives, in the classic style of its rival the LNWR which had just taken over the Pontardulais to Swansea line from the Llanelly Railway. The Midland's access to this system was via running powers over a branch of the Neath & Brecon Railway from Colbren to Ynisygeinon. This had been built jointly by the SVR and the N&BR in 1869, but afterwards vested in the latter company.

The original line of the SVR was along the eastern side of the valley. Such was the growth of industry in the lower part of the valley that the section between Upper Bank and Glais was duplicated through Morriston and Clydach along the western side. It was along this loop that the GWR chose to challenge the Midland. Its Morriston branch, later extended to Felin Fran, ran within yards of the Midland line for much of its length. It was along this loop too that the Midland ran its passenger services, both local and long-distance, the older direct line between Upper Boat and Glais which connected with the South Wales main line being reserved for freight.

Although part of a through route, as noted in Chapter 2, the Midland did not develop it to anything like its full potential. As a result the line from Swansea (St Thomas) to Colbren, with its branch to Brynamman never grew beyond a local valley railway. Neither the Midland, and later the LMS, did much to encourage local passenger traffic, the stations remaining small with usually only a single platform, devoid of any cover. At Brynamman where an end-on connection was made with the GWR each company built its own station on either side of a road bridge. The contrast between them was interesting, the Midland terminus being much inferior to that of the Great Western.

The Brynamman branch, running up the narrow, twisting and wooded valley of the Afon Twrch, before climbing to the bare moorland above Cwmllynfell, could have formed a connecting route with the branch from Pantyffynon. Perversely, the Midland station was built on a dead-end spur, even though the GWR built its station on the connecting link between the two branches, immediately beyond the intervening road overbridge. Thus long-suffering through passengers had always to walk between the two stations.

Motive power for the Swansea valley and Brynamman lines was provided by two sheds, one at Upper Bank (north of St Thomas station in Swansea), and the other at Gurnos. In latter years locomotive stock changed little. Three class 1F 0–6–0Ts of 19th century vintage, supplemented by six class 3F 0–6–0Ts of LMS design (Jinties) usually sufficed. Only in the closing years did any significant alteration occur when GWR 57xx class 0–6–0PTs were drafted in to replace the older Midland locomotives.

### The Swansea & Mumbles Railway

The Oystermouth Railway was incorporated on 29 June 1804, opened in 1806, and carried the first fare-paying railway passengers in the world on 25 March 1807. Running along the

*Plates 21 and 22.* Busy branches. *Above*: Cymmer Afan, with GWR 2-6-2T No 5545 with a Bridgend–Abergwynfi train standing in the GWR station, behind which stands the R & SB station with its distinctive signal box. Note the lattice girder viaduct which carried the GWR link with the SWMR. *Below*: Former GWR 0-6-0PTs Nos 4612 and 9675 head a Monmouthshire Railway Society special on the Morriston branch in 1965. Behind are the Swansea Canal and the Landore Viaduct. (*R.O. Tuck*)

*Plates 23 and 24.* Viaduct varieties. *Above*: The lattice girders of Cymmer Viaduct carried the GWR over the Afan Valley, to join up with the SWMR. In the foreground is the trackbed of the former R & SBR. *Below*: The former Port Talbot Railway Pontrhydyfen Viaduct on the line from Tonygroes to Tonmawr was in red brick, dominating the valley and nearby village. (*J.H.R. Page*)

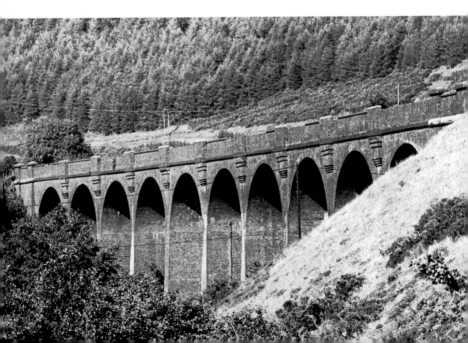

shore of Swansea Bay to Mumbles Pier (opened as late as 1898)
the line is best remembered by its later name of the Swansea
& Mumbles Railway, and that from 1929 motive power was by
large double-decker tramcars. This form of traction was the
fourth type used, others being horse, sail and steam. Although
only some five miles in length and relying for much of its life
only on passenger traffic, its history is remarkably complex. As
an example, its transformation from a horse-drawn tramway to
a railway was proposed in 1864, as an extension of the Neath &
Brecon Railway. The interested parties eventually gained control in 1877, only to find that the Swansea Improvements &
Tramway Company had obtained statutory running powers for
street tramway operation! The tramway company eventually
prevailed, and the line became in effect an extension of the Swansea street tram system, although its permanent way was built to
railway standards. The section east of the Rutland Street terminus escaped conversion, being eventually leased to the Swansea
Harbour Trust in 1897, and as a part of its system passed to the
Great Western Railway in 1923. Thus although appearing to be
isolated it was in fact connected to the Swansea rail
system as the latter developed by this extension eastwards from
Rutland Street (SS 657926), joining the LNWR just outside
Victoria station, and the Swansea Harbour Trust system near
the North Dock.

## West of the Loughor

Apart from the Dafen branch which was the first railway opened
by the Llanelly Railway Company in 1833, and the dock lines,
the rail network of Llanelly has remained remarkably intact.
The former branch followed a straight line for much of its
course north of the GWR main line, which it crossed on the level,
and served Dafen quietly and largely unnoticed for 136 years.
Its trackbed continues to serve the community as a series of useful footpaths linking modern housing estates and older communities on the eastern edge of Llanelly.

Straggling into Llanelly from the west came the Sandy
Junction branch of that interesting little company, the Burry
Port & Gwendraeth Valley Railway, once well-known for the

restricted dimensions of its passenger stock. This offshoot of the main BP&GVR system swung westward from Sandy Junction on the Llanelly & Mynydd Mawr Railway's branch to Cross Hands. It then ran parallel with the Great Western main line, from which it could be seen for much of its course, until making connection with it about 100yds east of Pembrey signal box. Originally it crossed the main line on the level and connected directly with sidings that served Burry Port harbour. Evidence of this crossing can still be found. To the north of the main line are the gateposts from which once hung the gate that guarded the exit from the branch, and to the south the line of the fence posts indicates the course of its one-time link to the nearby sidings.

Up to 1984 the main line of the BP&GVR remained intact until the opening of the branch to Coedbach Washery, north east of Kidwelly. The line is built partially on the site of the BP&GVR harbour branch together with a section of its neighbour the Gwendraeth Valley Railway. As a result of the opening of this new branch the BP&GVR line between Burry Port and the site of Kidwelly Junction was closed. Details of these lines will be found in the Postscript immediately preceeding the gazetteer.

# CHAPTER 10

# Carmarthen

Today the region beyond Carmarthen is best known for tourism and dairy farming. However the first railway built in this area, the narrow gauge Saundersfoot Railway, originally opened in 1832, was built to serve collieries around Saundersfoot. This aside, railway promotion in West Wales was undertaken for a multiplicity of reasons. In the minds of their original promoters one was conceived as a link to Ireland and the United States, two were to provide outlets for local quarries and lead mines, one merely to allow the expansion of a local harbour, and two to give Carmarthen direct links to the Midlands and the North. Politics, lack of finance and local support altered the aims, and sometimes even destinations of all in the course of time, and resulted in the rural network (the GWR main line excepted) that has suffered total annihilation in recent years.

During construction of the South Wales Railway westward from Carmarthen to New Milford (later renamed Neyland) which was completed in 1856, Cardigan recognised the benefits of a connection to it, and 1854 saw the promotion of the broad gauge Carmarthen & Cardigan Railway. Hopes of reaching Cardigan faded after completion to Llandyssul in 1864, although the GWR which leased the company in 1881, eventually extended the line to Newcastle Emlyn. Cardigan's salvation eventually came in 1866 with the opening of the Whitland & Cardigan Railway.

In 1864 the C&C was joined at Abergwili Junction by the standard gauge branch of the Llanelly Railway from Llandilo (operated by the LNWR from 1871), thus bringing the problems of the break of gauge to Carmarthen. In 1866 that extraordinary company, the Manchester & Milford Railway, gained

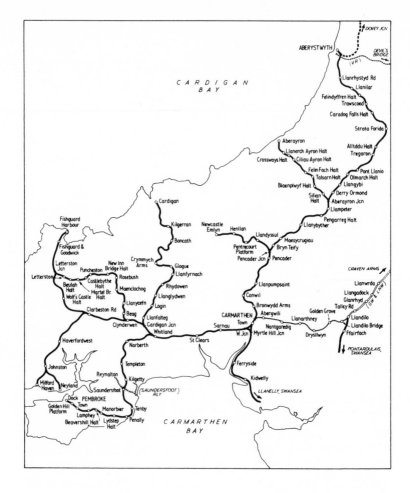

access to the town, following the laying of a third rail from
Pencader Junction to Abergwili Junction. The M&M had been
authorised in 1860 to build a line from Llanidloes to Pencader
as the 'missing link' in the chain of railways to be used to link
Manchester and Milford Haven. It eventually connected with
the Cambrian Railways at Aberystwyth in 1867, having abandoned a short section near Llangurig which was described in
*Forgotten Railways: North and Mid Wales*. The only addition
to this lonely line came in 1911 with the opening of the Lampeter, Aberayron & New Quay Light Railway. The final railway
to reach Carmarthen, in 1868, and which has survived as the
Pembroke Dock branch, was the Pembroke & Tenby Railway.

Completion of the rail network in West Wales centred around the North Pembroke & Fishguard Railway, which left the main line west of Clynderwen. Before completion, following its approaches to the LNWR, a concerned GWR bought and completed it. This involvement rekindled the urge in the GWR to develop Fishguard, resulting in an extension of the main line from Clarbeston Road to Letterston Junction on the NP&F, over which access was gained to Fishguard. Work was completed in 1906 with the opening of the present harbour, which although under threat of closure remains open for Irish traffic.

## North of Carmarthen

The end of an era came on the 30th September 1973 when the last train left the Felin Fran creamery for Lampeter and Carmarthen. Although not built specifically for milk traffic, prodigious quantities of this liquid were conveyed over the years. At Carmarthen it would be attached to similar loads emanating from further west before despatch to London and other places. As a boy I well remember seeing the 3.50pm Whitland–Kensington milk train, perhaps Castle-hauled, speeding eastwards through Cardiff, and if one had time to wait one could see a returning empties working. This would be milk and fish empties combined, for in the 1950s Milford Haven had a thriving fishing fleet, and it would be hauled by a Neyland County class 4–6–0, (*County of*) *Bucks*, *Monmouth* or *Worcester*, perhaps, striding westward into the sunset of an autumn evening.

Three railway companies built the lines north of Carmarthen, the C&C, the M&M, and lastly the LA&NQ and none of them ever succeeded in reaching all the towns in their titles. In fact the M&M never got within 140 miles of Manchester. The main branch was from Carmarthen to Aberystwyth, off which the smaller branches from Pencader and Lampeter, served Newcastle Emlyn and Aberayron respectively. All were single lines. The establishment of the main route over the tracks built by two different companies followed the absorption of the M&M by the GWR in 1911, up until when it had only worked the C&C line to Newcastle Emlyn.

Serious development of the Aberystwyth line for through traffic was hampered by the lightly-laid track, a state of affairs that only changed slowly, since traffic never warranted immediate upgrading. Until the late 1920s only 'uncoloured' locomotives, for example Dean Goods 0–6–0s, and Stella class 2–4–0s, along with a number of small tank engine classes, could work the traffic. Later all the branches were upgraded to 'blue' routes, thus allowing traffic to be worked by 43xx 2–6–0s and Manor class 4–6–0s. Like many branches elsewhere, passenger traffic tended to be hauled by regular locomotives, 'old faithfuls' whose occasional visits to works were greeted with dismay in case they never returned. 5819 (a 58xx 0–4–2T) was the regular passenger locomotive on the Newcastle Emlyn branch for many years. Overnight it would be stabled in the single-road shed at the end of the branch, with its thoughtfully provided turntable on the approach road.

Travelling from Carmarthen to Aberystwyth one was always struck by the loneliness of the line, and that once one had swung north at Abergwili Junction officialdom was far away and time ceased to have such pressing importance. Travelling behind a 43xx 2–6–0 in a compartment of a three-coach train one would compose oneself for some $2\frac{1}{2}$ hours travel to cover 56 miles.

Beyond Abergwili Junction where the Llandilo branch diverged to the east, one entered the narrow but beautifully wooded Gwili valley. This tortuous stream was followed past Bronwydd Arms (now the headquarters of the Gwili Railway Company which operates a steam service of Llwyfan Cerrig) and climbed steadily through Conwil and on to Llanpumpsaint. Only the platform faces remain of this one-time passing place. From here the climb continued to the sharpening bark of the 43xx, along the narrow Nantaeron, a tributary of the Gwili, until the 985yd Alltwalis tunnel was reached. Beyond came a brisk descent to Pencader, the junction for the branch to Newcastle Emlyn. Pencader was a delightful station, conveniently situated in the village. A well-proportioned single-storey building stood on the down platform, whilst on the southern end of the opposite platform was situated a substantial signalbox controlling the crossing loop and adjacent yard.

Once clear of Pencader Junction there followed a stiff climb before the descent into the broad Teifi valley which was followed to Lampeter. This stretch along the beautiful meandering river was delightful. Lampeter's fine stone station buildings and goods shed have survived the years. They are dilapidated, but their charm and elegance survive. North of Lampeter the line ran along one of the Teifi's tributaries, the Afon Dulas, which parallels the main river. Shortly after Olmarch Halt the line descended again to the broadening Teifi valley to pass through Tregaron and stride on a low embankment across Tregaron bog to Strata Florida.

From here it had been the intention of the M&M to head across the hills via Ysbyty Ystwyth and Devil's Bridge to join its isolated section at Llangurig, and hence gain the Mid Wales Railway. Instead, at Strata Florida, named after the nearby Abbey, the line swung sharply to the west and began climbing steeply out of the Vale of the Teifi. Strata Florida delightfully illustrates the perverseness that sometimes accompanied the naming of country stations. The nearest hamlet was Ystrad Meurig about a ½-mile west, the village of Pontrhydfendigaid lay two miles to the east. Strata Florida Abbey was a further 1½ miles beyond. One of the most interesting stretches of this branch could be seen looking south from the descending approach road to the station. With the surrounding hills pressed away to east and west, the line from Carmarthen came across the broad Tregaron bog as straight as an arrow, then when only a few yards away swung suddenly to the west to head away towards Aberystwyth. On a clear day a train would be in sight for ten minutes or more as it slowly crossed the bog before squealing to a halt at this isolated station.

Climbing and twisting to beyond Trawscoed, which commanded fine views to north and east, the branch now descended to the Afon Ystwyth for the final nine miles to Aberystwyth. The 56 miles from Carmarthen were a delight of changing scenes as one ran along one or other river or climbed across the hills that separated them, but it was always something of a relief to reach here after more than 2½ hours.

Carmarthen trains used the bay platform on the south side

of the station, and approached around a sharp curve. Since closure, this bay has found a new use, happily a railway one. Some years ago the Vale of Rheidol narrow-gauge railway, British Rail's only steam-powered branch, was diverted into it. The bay now serves as a terminus for this line, and the adjacent shed that once held Dukedogs and Manors, those doyens of the Shrewsbury to Aberystwyth line, now houses the three narrow-gauge locomotives of the V of R.

If travel on the Carmarthen to Aberystwyth line was leisurely, that on the Aberayron branch was even slower. The reason was not hard to find—level crossings. In its $13\frac{1}{2}$-mile length the branch had no less than twelve, and one stretch contained three in the space of 1200yds. This branch epitomised the importance of the milk traffic to the railways in the region. Opened in 1911, passenger traffic ceased in May 1951, after 40 years in all. However, milk traffic to the creamery at Felin Fach, about half-way along the branch, kept the line alive until September 1973, a further 22 years.

### The Llandilo branch

Carmarthen was the most westerly point reached by the LNWR in South Wales. The single line from Llandilo was built by the Llanelly Railway and opened to Abergwili Junction on the C&C in 1864. Running powers over the latter took it into Carmarthen. The North Western started working the line in 1871, and the Llanelly company eventually sold it to them in 1873, withdrawing completely from the branch the following year. How the inept Llanelly company lost out to the LNWR has been related in Chapter 9.

Running along the broad valley of the Twyi, this pretty little branch served the useful purpose of linking Carmarthen and Llandilo, thus giving the former town a direct link to the Midlands. It is rather surprising that having reached the town, albeit in a somewhat unorthodox fashion, the LNWR never worked through services off the Central Wales line, always treating it merely as a branch feeder. Even though it was a line of humble status, this did not stop the North Western lavishing money upon it. At every station it built a series of soundly constructed charmingly proportioned buildings in local stone.

To travel the branch was to savour the delights of a country railway, something of a rarity in South Wales. The journey, which took about 45 minutes, delighted a traveller as the line ran alongside the meandering Twyi, contriving to cross it only once, although a second bridge crossed a tributary. The valley is broad and picturesque for the whole length of the branch, and only narrows for a short distance to the west of the knoll on which broods the ruins of Drysllwyn castle.

Today, some 24 years after the closure of the branch on 9 September 1963, it is surprising to find so much still remaining. Every station building except Llandilo Bridge has survived to be converted into a private house, and even the goods shed at Nantgaredig still stands alongside the road here. Whilst many have been modified, Nantgaredig station for example, all retain their simple elegance. A particularly fine and unaltered station is Golden Grove (SN 590211), where one can also find a complete LNWR starter signal.

### The Cardigan branch

From Cardigan Junction, $2\frac{1}{4}$ miles west of Whitland, the $25\frac{1}{4}$-mile branch swung north and by a most tortuous route eventually reached Cardigan. At first it ran along the valley of the Taf, which although thickly wooded in its lower part became more austere as one passed the disused lead mine at Llanfyrnach and the slate quarry at Glogue. The branch climbed beyond the river near the latter's source at Crymmych Arms, whence it gained the high ground along the eastern foothills of the Prescelli range. Beyond, a steep twisting descent brought it to the Teifi near Kilgerran, from where a short run led to Cardigan.

Originally constructed to serve the lead mine and slate quarry, the branch is now recalled as a quiet country byway, with a leisurely journey time of about $1\frac{1}{2}$ hours. This time was reputedly extended on numerous occasions if a suitable rabbit or pheasant was unfortunate enough to come within shotgun range of the track.

As the Whitland & Taf Vale Railway the branch opened in March 1873 and was later extended to Crymmych Arms. Shortly afterwards it achieved a certain notoriety in official circles by opening to passengers on 12 July 1875 without Board of Trade inspection or approval. This was due to the failure of the inspecting officer to conduct his inspection within the period prescribed following notification of the company's intention. Steps were soon taken to extend the line to Cardigan. Acts of 1877 and 1883 authorised the extension, together with a change of name to the Whitland & Cardigan Railway, and provided for the GWR to work the line following the completion to Cardigan. This it did from 1 September 1886. The W&C was finally absorbed into the Great Western in July 1890.

Although closed completely in May 1963 the branch has refused to fade away. Six of the ten stations remain, all in private hands. The atmosphere of the branch can now be best recalled at Crymmych Arms and Cardigan. Crymmych Arms, although partially altered, has retained all its main features on both platforms, except the signalbox. The site is somewhat cramped and it is difficult to imagine the scene common in years gone by on market days. On such days (once a month) a cattle, horse and sheep fair was held in the village. For this event a special train would be run from Carmarthen, which prior to World War II would frequently be headed by Dean Goods 0–6–0s which were the only tender locomotives to work on the line.

Finally there is Cardigan, situated on the south bank of the Teifi on the outskirts of the town. Only the signalbox and locomotive shed have been demolished. Both stood at the east end of the station, the former on the single platform, the latter near the river bank. Although now used by a local agricultural merchant the station building survives intact, even to the platform awning. The substantial stone goods shed stands opposite. Despite the removal of the tracks and the buildings mentioned it is surprising how it retains its country station atmosphere. Scenes, gilded in hindsight by eternal summer, spring quickly to mind after a few moments on the deserted platform—well-tended flower beds, and a sparkle of sunlight on the river. A bell rings in the signalbox, to be followed by the click of a moving point, and the crash of a moving signal arm. A whistle sound follows and a train bustles in and people busy themselves. Such a scene would have been possible in 1958, 1948 or before. It is a pity it cannot be repeated in 1988.

### The Saundersfoot Railway

Saundersfoot is today a small seaside resort whose livelihood depends upon the tourist trade. It is now hard to believe that the harbour was built for coal exporting, and that the town once had close links with France, Spain and Prussia.

To develop the mining interests in this area of Pembrokeshire the Saundersfoot Railway & Harbour Company was incorporated in 1828 to build a harbour and connecting tramway via an inclined plane to collieries at Thomas Chapel. This line opened in 1832 and a branch to Wiseman's Bridge and Kilgetty along the coast, partially through tunnels beneath the cliffs, was opened about 1843. Short extensions were added over the years, the last being in 1915 to Reynalton 1½ miles west of Thomas Chapel.

What set this railway apart, and ensured its total isolation from the main rail network, which it passed beneath near Saundersfoot station on the Pembroke Dock branch, was its peculiar gauge. For reasons now lost forever a gauge of 4ft was officially selected, but in practice this varied between 4ft and 4ft ¾in. In addition, the method of working was somewhat unusual. Steam traction came to the line in 1874 in the shape of a Manning Wardle 0–4–0T, which could only operate to the foot of the incline on the route to Thomas Chapel. It was not until 1915, following the extension to Reynalton that a steam locomotive was used on the upper section. This was a diminutive Kerr Stuart 0–4–0ST which, to pass through the tunnel beneath Saundersfoot station, was restricted to an overall height of only 6ft 0in.

This unique little line closed in 1939, after the last colliery ceased operation. Developments particularly related to the road-oriented tourist industry have obliterated much of the old railway, except for the tunnels. These have been incorporated into the coast path that leads northwards to Wiseman's Bridge.

## Neyland

The line from Johnston to Neyland is the only part of the Great Western main line in South Wales to have suffered closure. Selected by Brunel as the terminus of the South Wales Railway, a tightly-knit but proud and independent railway community grew up on the northern shores of Milford Haven. To them Paddington was 'the other end of the line.' Even though it lost its position as the terminus for the Irish traffic following the opening of Fishguard Harbour in 1906, it continued to be served directly from Paddington for over half a century more. A regular feature of this service were the sleeping car trains, typically departing at 6.30pm for Paddington, the balancing working arriving at 6.39am.

Now only trackbed remains, running south-east from Johnston and terminating at a wide shelf at the very edge of the Haven. This once proud and busy terminus has been laid flat, and the whistle shrieks that heralded the departure of the 1.00pm to London, the 9.00am railmotor to Clarbeston Road, or a shunting movement in the sidings no longer startle the seagulls.

## The slow route to Fishguard

Only for those travelling westward by rail who know where the precise place $1\frac{1}{4}$ miles west of Clynderwen, and who can also discern the traces of an abandoned railway, is it possible to spot where the Letterston branch diverged from the South Wales main line. From here the 17-mile branch across the Prescelli hills swung northwards to serve Maenclochog, Rosebush and Letterston before rejoining the main line at Letterston Junction.

Like the Cardigan branch to the east, the line began life as a mineral railway. Unlike that branch, however, very little has survived. As the Narberth Road & Maenclochog Railway it was opened in 1876 to slate quarries at Rosebush, high in the bare Prescelli hills. Following the decision to extend the line to Fishguard the story of the line ceases to be straightforward. Suffice to say that the antics of this little company, by now known as the North Pembroke & Fishguard Railway, threw such a fright into the GWR by approaching the LNWR and offering it an alternative route to Ireland, that in 1898 the GWR bought it out shortly before construction was completed. In 1906 the branch west of Letterston was incorporated into the new line to Fishguard from Clarbeston Road.

From that date the branch became a rural backwater, and would have had little further to commend it to memory had it not been for the indignities heaped upon it. The branch was closed between 1882 and 1895, and before its final demise, ceased operating in both World Wars. Further indignities were to follow. After closure in 1917 the track was lifted and shipped to France, but it never arrived due to enemy action.

But the unkindest cut of all came during World War II when the branch earned the doubtful distinction of being the only UK railway to be bombed and strafed—by the Allies! During 1943 and 1944 locomotives were towed on to the line and used by the RAF and USAF for target practice, for at this time disruption of the German railway system was high on the Allies' list of priorities. In addition, Maenclochog tunnel was also used for target practice for the bouncing bombs invented by the late Sir Barnes Wallis. That the branch survived all this to re-open again, albeit in two sections (but including the tunnel) was remarkable. The section from Whitland to Puncheston only survived until 1949, but the short length to Letterston from the nearby junction remained open until 1965.

## The lasting memories

Now this branch, like so many others is merely a fading memory, and the railway scene is the poorer for their passing. The density of railways in South Wales made it unique in Great Britain, if not the world. In its heyday the traffic was sufficient to require over 1700 steam locomotives, many of which were stationed on the lines that are now closed. At the time their daily passage went largely unnoticed, so taken for granted were they. Today the car and lorry are equally taken for granted. In, say, 50 years' time will these too be remembered with equal affection?—Perhaps.

# Postscript

## *The Toll of The Eighties*

In the nine years since the first edition of this book was published the economic recession of the early eighties and the subsequent retrenchment of South Wales' staple industries, steel and, in particular, coal, have had their inevitable effect upon the railways of the area. Although not as sweeping as the closures of twenty five years or so ago, when an axe was summarily put to many a route or branch, the remaining lines may truthfully be said to be suffering death by a thousand cuts. Amongst the valleys that have now lost their railways entirely are the Tawe, Neath, Ogmore, Garw and, unbelievable only a few years ago, the Rhondda Fach. Many of the remaining valley lines have now been shortened as for example in the Rhymney, where the old Brecon & Merthyr line now terminates at Machen Quarry. Elsewhere further shortening of branches has taken place, but perhaps the most noticeable closures, although strictly outside the scope of this book, have been the withdrawal of facilities on the remaining network, particularly the main line. Ebbw Junction and Severn Tunnel Junction motive power depots have closed, and the number of local stabling points has been reduced. The rail networks in and to the remaining South Wales docks are small and ever reducing as road transport takes an increasing share of what little traffic remains. But perhaps the most dramatic example of this trend can be seen at the now empty gateway to South Wales – Severn Tunnel Junction yards.

Yet strangely there is another side to the coin; the bustling passenger traffic on those valley lines fortunate enough to have retained such services. Revenue has increased dramatically in recent years, leading to the opening of new stations as at Ynyswen in the Rhondda valley, the re-introduction on a limited scale of passenger services in the Cynon valley, and even the opening of a new line to passengers. This is the ex-Taff Vale Railway mineral line between Radyr and Penarth Curve North Junction, and was heralded as the first such opening in South Wales for 75 years. Replacement of ageing D M U sets by 'Sprinters' has recently taken place, and the local British Rail management is confident that local passenger traffic will continue to increase.

Much has therefore happened since the first edition and this Postcript brings together the major closures that have occurred during this time, describing each, broadly in geographical order from east to west, in line with the layout of chapters 3 to 10.

### Pontypool and Abergavenny

As mentioned on page 41 the valley of the Afon-lwyd and its tributaries are narrow and steep sided even by South Wales standards. Incline planes were common, which severely restricted attempts to develop collieries in this area. Thus in 1874 the GWR obtained powers to build a new line from Trevethin Junction, north of Pontypool, to collieries in the Abersychan and Talywain area, high in the hills to the west of the Afon-lwyd. Apart from the desire to develop the collieries of the Afon-lwyd by allowing better access, which this branch satisfied by providing a more uniformly graded, if somewhat tortuous exit southwards to Pontypool or Newport, there was a second reason for the GWR building the line. This was political, the branch effectively forestalling the advance of the LNWR. Thus that company's influence was limited to the remote windswept uplands towards the top of the valley. Its revenge came two years later, however, when its acquisition of the Sirhowy Railway gave it access to Newport and a further toe-hold in the South Wales export coal trade.

The branch diverged sharply westward from Trevethin Junction. At first hugging the hillside, and climbing steeply, it soon swung in a great semi-circle on a high embankment above both the Cwmffrwdoer and Cwmnantddu branches, to face east before finally swinging northwards. Heavy earthworks followed across barren uplands before Golynos was reached, and a spur, some 800 yards to the south, to Abersychan & Talywain, made an end on connection to the LNWR.

### Newport

Until quite recently, of the lines radiating into the valleys from Newport, that to the Ebbw, the Western Valley as it is known locally, survived virtually intact, having suffered only the loss of short sections of its northern extremities.

The greatest of these recent losses is the six mile branch from Aberbeeg to Nantyglo, opened by the Monmouthshire Railway & Canal Company in 1824 as a tramroad off a similar line from Crumlin to Beaufort that had already been in use for 26 years.

Along with the other MR & CC tramroads in the Western Valley
it was converted to a railway in 1855. The branch commenced at
Aberbeeg, and although the station, which had Up and Down
platforms on both the lines to Nantyglo and Ebbw Vale, stood
right at the junction, its name never reflected its status. The only
concession made by officialdom was in the nameboards, which
on the Nantyglo side read: 'Aberbeeg – Change for Ebbw Vale',
whilst on the Ebbw Vale side read: 'Aberbeeg – Change for
Brynmawr'.

As one travelled along the branch, Six Bells Colliery was soon
passed, together with the Halt opened in 1937, which despite its
wooden buildings and humble status was provided with an
awning that would not have disgraced many a larger station. The
line swung to the north beyond here and keeping to the narrow
valley floor passed through Abertillery, Bournville, and Blaina
before finally reaching Nantyglo. From here the line continued
over LNWR/GWR joint metals to Brynmawr. Both Abertillery
and Blaina had large solidly built stone station buildings on the
Up platform, and at the latter the signal box too stood on the Up
platform. The branch lost its passenger service in 1962, and was
gradually shortened as colliery closures occurred, the last section
being taken out of use following the shut down of Six Bells
colliery in 1986. Beyond Six Bells the railway site is now, or
shortly will be, incorporated into a new road running the length
of the valley. At Abertillery a short mineral branch ran to
Cwmtillery. Less than a mile long it opened in 1858 and closed in
1963.

In the Ebbw Fawr two closures have occurred in the last few
years. The line beyond the southern end of the Ebbw Vale
steelworks, which once ran to Ebbw Vale (Low Level) (a small
single platform station with an attractive brick station building
opening directly on to the road that ran alongside) succumbed a
little at a time between 1962 and 1977. A short extension once
ran to the Beaufort Ironworks, but this length was out of use by
1939. The second closure was towards the southern end of the
valley. This was the Cwmcarn branch, a 72 chain mineral line
opened in 1911 and closed in 1978.

The junction for the Cwmcarn branch actually turned
eastwards not off the MR & CC line but from what had
originally been Hall's Tramroad. This line had a very chequered
and rather obscure history until the early years of this century
when in 1912, following many years of delay after the GWR had
obtained a lease, it was re-opened again throughout as a railway
running from Halls Road Junction to Markham Colliery. (It had

*Plates 25 and 26.* The Swindon touch. *Above*: Former Taff Vale Class A 0-6-2 T, as BR No 384, near Blaenrhondda on the R & SB line. Note the early BR lion and wheel emblem. *Below*: Ex-GWR 2-8-0T No 5216 shunts at Duffryn Yard, near Port Talbot. (*Brian Moone*)

Plates 27 and 28. In quiet byways. *Above*: 'Local inhabitants' hold up passenger and freight trains crossing at Llanglydwen on the Whitland–Cardigan branch in 1960. *Below*: Ex-GWR 0-6-0PT No 7407 pauses at Felin Fach with a class C milk and parcels train on the Aberayron branch in 1959. (*R.O. Tuck*)

been opened as a tramroad about 1805). Still known today as Halls Tramroad, having diverged on the east side of the Western Valley line, it soon rises steeply and swings across the valley. Continuing northwards it turns north-west near Llanhilleth, piercing the ridge to the Sirhowy valley, where it once made a connection at Penar Junction with the Pontypool to Neath line, then swings north again along the eastern slopes of the Sirhowy to Markham Colliery. Surviving a brief closure between Penar Junction and its junction with the Western Valley line, it remained in full use until 1979 when the length from Oakdale to Markham collieries was closed following the latter's demise.

## Cardiff and Barry

A number of closures in the Rhondda valleys have now taken place of which the most notable, the Rhondda Fach branch, is the most recent. Diverging northwards at Porth this branch ran by way of Ynyshir, Tylorstown, and Ferndale to Maerdy and beyond to the colliery of the same name. Opened in stages between 1849 and 1877 it was regarded by the Taff Vale Railway very much as a mineral branch, the local inhabitants having to wait until 1876 for the opening of a passenger service, which even then only ran as far as Ferndale. It was another thirteen years before it was extended to Maerdy. By contrast the passenger service had reached the head of the Rhondda Fawr by 1863. A narrow twisting steeply graded valley line, its operating difficulties were compounded by re-occurring subsidence that made a mockery of official line gradients. That this was so is not so surprising perhaps when one recalls that in its heyday this valley supported over twenty collieries, of which no less than nine were concentrated in about 1½ miles between Tylorstown and Ferndale. The passenger services that once served substantial and rather attractive stations (Maerdy excepted), were withdrawn in 1964. Over the years, as elsewhere, the collieries were closed one by one until finally only Maerdy remained. This lifted its last coal on 30 June 1986, and the branch closed a few weeks later.

Of the remaining Taff Vale Railway lines in the Rhondda that are now closed, the Eirw branch was little more than a siding leading to Cymmer colliery, whilst the other casualty was the east-to-north connection to the Taff valley near Pontypridd (between Rhondda Cutting Junction and North Curve Junction). Elsewhere in the area the Taff valley has lost the short branch to Nantgarw colliery, built partially on the line of the ill-

starred Cardiff Railway, and although not yet closed, the recent
announcement of the intended closure of the Lady Windsor
Colliery at Ynysybwl spells the end of the branch, opened in
1886, from Stormstown Junction.

Arguably of the South Wales railway companies the Rhymney
Railway has most successfully survived the line closures of the
last three decades. It has lost its 'Joint Lines' (with the GWR to
Merthyr, and the LNWR to Rhymney Bridge), but its main line
remains intact, unlike that of its one-time rival the B&M, and is
enjoying a revival in passenger numbers. Even its coal traffic is
quite healthy, although one must be careful with such a
statement and qualify it by adding – in March 1988, at the time
of writing – since it still serves two collieries and an opencast site.

The closures of recent years have been in the Caerphilly area.
The first to close, in May 1967, was the direct connection
between Caerphilly West Junction and Penrhos Junction,
together with the Beddau Loop, which had been made redundant following the ending of goods services from Penrhos
Junction to Glyntaff in January of that year. Ten years later this
closure was followed by that of the Senghenydd branch from
Aber Junction. Opened in 1894, this single line branch ran into
the steeply sided valley running north-west from Caerphilly to
the Windsor Colliery at Senghenydd, at the valley's end.
Senghenydd station, which closed when the passenger service
was withdrawn in 1964, with its curved single platform and small
stone-built buildings, always had a slightly forlorn look about it.
The branch finally succumbed in 1977.

The final member of a trio of closures is a section of the
Rhymney Railway's original main line from Aber Junction to
Walnut Tree Junction in the Taff valley, the steep bank between
Penrhos and the Taff Vale being invariably referred to locally as
the 'Big Hill'. From 1858 to 1871 it was the only means of access
that the RR had to the docks at Cardiff, and for many years was a
source of friction between these two companies, the RR
continually complaining of delays to its traffic. Throughout its
existence the RR maintained an engine shed at the junction
which can still be seen on the site of a nearby works.

### Llantrisant and Bridgend

In recent years the branches to both Nantymoel and Blaengarw
have succumbed to the accelerating decline of coal mining in
South Wales. Opened in 1865 and 1876 respectively these once
busy lines, along with that in the nearby Llynfi valley, were

instrumental in making Tondu one of the most important junctions in the South Wales valleys. In fact a Traffic Control Office was set up here by the GWR, and survived until quite recently. Sheltered beneath the terraces of the villages they served, their single platform termini, with their rather small but neat wooden buildings, last saw passenger services in 1958 and 1953 respectively, though the coal traffic in these valleys continued until 1986.

## Swansea to Llanelly

East of Kidwelly station there once existed the junction of the Gwendraeth Valley Railway. For many years all traces of this, as well as the nearby Burry Port & Gwendraeth Valley Railway branch to Kidwelly harbour that once passed beneath the South Wales main line, had disappeared. But in 1983 British Rail opened a line to the NCB washery at Coedbach. To do this they utilised a short length of the GVR between the sites of the main line junction and Tycoch Junction, whilst from there to Coedbach they utilised a length of the BP&GVR branch. The GVR was owned by (but not merged with) the Kidwelly Tinplate Company, which purchased it from a receiver in 1910 as an outlet to the main line. As well as the tinplate works it also served a silica brick works and limekilns. North of Kidwelly it was connected to the harbour branch of its neighbour. This latter ran to a riverside quay and small basin. However, the shallows of the Gwendraeth estuary ensured that it was doomed to failure, and it closed in the 1930s. This connection between the two railways ensured that a small section of the GVR remained open long after the closure of the remainder of the line. It was, in fact, the only access by which a breakdown crane could reach the BP&GVR system, since the low bridge at Burry Port that was responsible for the restricted size of the passenger stock was too small for the crane.

Apart from this the GVR is noteworthy for harbouring, for many years within the ruins of the tinplate works, the Fox Walker 0-6-0ST that it had purchased from the GWR in 1910. This had come originally from the North Pembroke & Fishguard Railway, the impecunious little line in the far west whose story was told in Chapter 10. Happily this locomotive has been preserved at the Pembroke County Museum at Scolton Park.

The rebuilding of the GVR line had an unfortunate effect upon its neighbour however, since it precipitated the closure of a section of the 'main line' of the BP&GVR. This was from Burry

Port to Kidwelly Junction, across the flat featureless lowland at the entrance to the Gwendraeth valley. But its closure was a blessing to the operating authorities as it at long last removed the clearance restrictions imposed by the bridge near Burry Port that had always bedevilled the working of this line.

The closure of this section of the BP&GVR took place on 17 September 1983 and it is fitting to recall here that the closure of a branch from it had occurred as far back as 1957, although the exact date seems not to have been recorded. The branch was for minerals only and ran from Trimsaran Junction to a colliery at Trimsaran. It was opened in 1873.

### Carmarthen

The catalogue of closures in South Wales as line after line fell to the axe of harsh economic reality was, to a very limited extent, balanced in the Milford Haven area by the construction in the sixties and seventies of branches to serve the then rapidly expanding oil industry. Refineries were built along the northern shore of the Haven at Herbranston, Robeston, and Waterston, and lines from the Milford Haven branch were constructed to them. But with the violent reversals in fortunes of the oil industry, the Esso refinery at Herbranston is now closed, as is the short branch that served it, and which had a life of less than 24 years. By way of contrast the nearby Johnston to Neyland branch was in use for 108 years, and it is interesting to recall that the last line built by the GWR to serve the coalfield, that from Clydach-on-Tawe to Trebanos, and opened as late as 1923, remained in use for 41 years. By South Wales standards the track on the Herbranston branch at its closure was scarely bedded in!

# Gazetteer

## BRECON

To search for Brecon's railways within the town itself is not a rewarding affair. Brecon has completely turned its back on that phase of its history. To search within the county, and its easterly neighbour, is hardly less rewarding. Nature and the farmer are reclaiming their lost lands. Reminders of the spirit and tenacity of the generation that attempted to bring the advantages of rail transport to the county are best seen in the mountains south of Brecon. Here in the thin upland soil the paths of the railways remain clearly etched, mute reminders of earlier visions.

BRECON–DOWLAIS (PANT)                                          19 miles
*Brecon & Merthyr Tydfil Junction Railway*
*ACTS* : 1 August 1859 (Talybont–Dowlais); 15 May 1860 (Brecon–Talybont).
*OPENED* : 23 April 1863 *(pass and gds)*.
*CLOSED* : 31 December 1962 *(pass)*; 4 May 1964 *(gds)*.
*REMAINS* : At the crossing of the river Usk at SO 122234 the base of the central pier remains. Talybont station building stands nearby at SO 117228. At Torpantau (SO 049168) only the outline of the platforms can be traced, but the southern end of the tunnel is accessible. South of here the trackbed can be followed to Pant station (SO 060096). Buildings remain at Pant, Ponsticill and Dolygaer (SO 058145).
*USES* : Tallyllyn station and adjacent tunnel are now privately-owned; the latter has been rebuilt and the platform area converted to a garden. Talybont and Dolygaer are used by separate local authorities as outdoor pursuit centres. The section from Pant to Torpantau has been leased from the Forestry Commission by Hills & Bailey Ltd who have opened the 2ft 0in gauge Brecon Mountain Railway between Pant and Ponsticill.

PONSTICILL JUNCTION–MERTHYR (RHYDYCAR JUNCTION)
6 miles 27 chains
*Brecon & Merthyr Tydfil Junction Railway (Joint with London & North Western Railway between Morlais Junction and Rhydycar Junction).*

*ACTS* : 28 July 1862 (Brecon & Merthyr); 19 July 1875 (London
& North Western powers to extend from Dowlais and make
the section between Morlais Junction and Rhydycar Junction
Joint).
*OPENED* : 1 August 1867 *(pass and gds)*; Ponsticill Junction–
Cefn. 1 August 1868 *(pass and gds)*; Cefn–Merthyr (Rhydycar
Junction).
*CLOSED* : 13 November 1961 *(pass)*; Ponsticill Junction–
Merthyr (Rhydycar Junction). 4 May 1964 *(gds)*: Ponsticill
Junction–Vaynor Quarry. 3 October 1966 *(gds)*: Vaynor
Quarry–Merthyr (Rhydycar Junction).
*REMAINS* : The line is easily traced running south on a falling
gradient unilt it swings west below Morlais quarry. The
outstanding features are the two beautiful stone viaducts at
Pontsarn (SO 046099) and Cefn Coed (SO 031077). A fine
place to view the latter is from the front of Cyfarthfa Castle
(SO 042074), which is now an interesting museum devoted to
Merthyr and Dowlais, and contains some fine exhibits of the
Dowlais Iron Company's railway products.

PANT–DOWLAIS CENTRAL (originally LLOYD STREET)          1¼ miles
*Brecon & Merthyr Tydfil Junction Railway*
*ACT* : 5 July 1865
*OPENED* : 23 June 1869 *(pass and gds)*
*CLOSED* : 2 May 1960 *(pass)*; 4 May 1964 *(gds)*
*REMAINS* : The trackbed can be traced from the site of Pant
station to a short way north of the site of Pantysgallog station.
At the branch terminus (SO 065080) only the station and
approach remain, south of the viaduct carrying the Heads of
the Valleys road. Central station buildings and goods shed still
stand atop an embankment jutting high out of the hillside and
which terminates in a steep drop a little beyond where the
buffers once stood.
*USES* : Road widening has claimed the trackbed between
Pantysgallog and the road viaduct. South of this a local
haulage firm occupies a length of the trackbed. The goods shed
is now a community centre.

BRECON–CRAIG-Y-NOS                                    18¾ miles
*Neath & Brecon Railway*
*ACT* : 13 July 1863
*OPENED* : 3 June 1867
*CLOSED* : 15 October 1962 *(pass and gds)* Onllwyn–Craig-y-Nos
remained open to goods from Neath until 7 October 1963; re-
opened for goods 1 July 1964; finally closed 16 November 1981.

*REMAINS* : A bridge abutment and earthworks running westward from SO 037290. The Usk was crossed at SN 947297 on the skew, the massive abutments and embankments remain here. The bridge over the A40 at Sennybridge (SN 926291) still retains the original abutments, but is now a road bridge. The trackbed can be followed from alongside Cray reservoir at SN 885217, for about 1½ miles southwards.

*USES* : Within Brecon two sections east of SO 037290 have been used for private housing developments. Northwards from Craig-y-Nos the trackbed is a walk in the Brecon Beacons National Park.

TALYLLYN JUNCTION–HEREFORD                34¼ miles
*Hereford Hay & Brecon Railway*
*ACTS* : 8 August 1859; 6 August 1860 (Transfer of Talyllyn—Three Cocks section to Mid Wales Railway, and Brecon—Talyllyn section to Brecon & Merthyr Railway); 30 July 1874 (Leased to Midland Railway, vested in that company 1886).
*OPENED* : 29 June 1863 *(pass and gds)*, Hereford–Eardisley; 11 July 1864 *(pass and gds)*, Eardisley–Hay; 1 September 1864 *(gds)*, 21 September 1864 *(pass)*, Hay–Brecon.
*CLOSED* : 31 December 1962 *(pass)* Talyllyn Junction–Hereford; 4 May 1964 *(gds)* Talyllyn Junction–Eardisley; 28 September 1964 *(gds)* Eardisley–Hereford (Brecon Junction); 1 August 1966 Hereford (Brecon Junction)–Hereford (Moorfields Junction).
*REMAINS* : The trackbed of this line can only be followed in isolated lengths, much of it now being overgrown, or in private hands, usually local farmers. Many examples of the line's single arch stone bridges remain, the most outstanding being near Glasbury, at SO 182391. Smaller examples can be found, all near the Hereford end of the line at SO 389469, SO 418446, SO 445429 and SO 467422. All bridges that remain intact between Glasbury and Norton Canon are of brick abutments with girder spans. There is one exception at SO 251468, where the line is still carried over a farm access road by a timber trestle bridge. Examples of station buildings can only be found at Three Cocks Junction, Hay, Eardisley and Kinnersley (a small store only). The site of the junction at Hereford (Moorfields) is easily traced.
*USES* : Three Cocks Junction is now a Calor Gas distribution depot, the station building being used as offices. Hay-on-Wye station is used jointly by builders and a timber merchant, and the Hay & District Farmers' Cooperative (which uses the goods shed). Eardisley station is now privately owned, some

original buildings remaining, notably the large brick goods shed. At Hereford the junction to Barton station is now the access to the Bulmer's Railway Centre, and the first ½-mile of the line is used by the locomotives housed here, when giving rides to the public.

# MONMOUTH

The completion of the railways linking Chepstow, Monmouth and Ross-on-Wye a little over a 100 years ago, effectively killed the river trade that had flourished for centuries before. In its turn the advent of road transport killed the railway, but unlike it, has failed to sustain or revitalise the valley's indigenous industries. Today the Wye valley is internationally renowned for its beauty, part of which can be seen to advantage by walking the three sections of closed railway, some four miles in total, that have been incorporated into public walks.

LITTLE MILL JUNCTION–MONMOUTH (TROY)          15 miles 69 chains
*Coleford, Monmouth, Usk & Pontypool Railway*
*ACT* : 20 August 1853
*OPENED* : 2 June 1856 *(pass and gds)* Little Mill-Usk; 12 October 1857 *(pass and gds)* Usk–Monmouth (Troy).
*CLOSED* : 30 May 1955 *(pass)* Little Mill Junction–Monmouth (Troy); 13 June 1955 *(gds)* Usk–Monmouth (Troy); 13 September 1965 *(gds)* Glascoed–Usk.
*REMAINS* : SO 373013, river bridge and adjacent road bridge (note the later brick and girder addition alongside the original sandstone bridge). SO 375013 Usk tunnel. SO 417041 Llandenny station buildings and signal box. SO 421075 Raglan station building. SO 460098 Dingstow station buildings. SO 509118 Monmouth (Troy). Here are the original station buildings, goods shed, and northern entrance to Troy tunnel.
*USES* : Almost the entire length of the branch from Usk to Monmouth has been incorporated into the A40/A449 road, whose twin tunnels at Monmouth pierce the hill a little to the north of the railway tunnel. Raglan station buildings are used for storage purposes by the Gwent County Council highways department. Monmouth (Troy) station site is rented to a local haulage contractor, and Dingstow to a farmers co-operative.

ROSS ON WYE–MONMOUTH (TROY)          13 miles 11 chains
*Ross & Monmouth Railway*
*ACT* : 28 July 1863

*OPENED* : 1 August 1873 *(pass and gds)*, Ross–Monmouth (May Hill); 1 May 1874 *(pass and gds)*, Monmouth (May Hill)–Monmouth (Troy).

*CLOSED* : 5 January 1959 *(pass)*, Ross–Monmouth (Troy); 2 November 1964 *(gds)*, Monmouth (Troy)–Lydbrook; 1 November 1965 *(gds)* Lydbrook–Ross.

*REMAINS* : Goods and engine sheds at Ross-on-Wye station site (SO 606244). Overbridge with brick parapet at SO 597232. Trackbed can be followed alongside B4228 from SO 584194 to the site of Kerne Bridge station at SO 581191. A river bridge can be crossed at SO 587177; a continuation of the footpath northwards leads to the southern portal of Bicknor tunnel. Looking south-east from Symonds Yat Rock (SO 564160) a section of trackbed can just be discerned in the trees alongside the near river bank, from SO 566158 to SO 571157. From Symonds Yat station site (SO 562158) the line can be traced as far as SO 549144. It can then be picked-up between the minor road and the river between SO 529148 and SO 517132. A sandstone bridge remains at SO 512127, and the route can be followed to the bowstring girder bridge across the Wye, and beyond to Monmouth (Troy) station.

*USES* : Ross-on-Wye station site is now a light industrial estate, as is the track immediately south of the nearby A40. Kerne Bridge station is privately owned, as is Symonds Yat tunnel. Symonds Yat station site is now partially used as a private car park, and the trackbed to the south, as far as SO 549144 is part of the Wye Valley Walk, and signposted as such. The site of Monmouth (May Hill) and the adjacent area (SO 513128) has been incorporated into a light industrial estate.

CHEPSTOW (WYE VALLEY JUNCTION)–MONMOUTH (TROY)
                                        13 miles 62 chains
*Coleford, Monmouth, Usk & Pontypool Railway* (Monmouth (Troy)–Wyesham Junction)
*Wye Valley Railway* (Wyesham Junction–Chepstow (Wye Valley Junction).)

*ACTS* : 20 August 1853 (Coleford, Monmouth, Usk & Pontypool Railway); 10 August 1866 (Wye Valley Railway).

*OPENED* : 1 July 1861 *(pass and gds)*, Monmouth (Troy)–Wyesham Junction; 1 November 1876 *(pass and gds)*, Wyesham Junction–Chepstow (Wye Valley Junction).

*CLOSED* : 5 January 1959 *(pass)*, Monmouth (Troy)–Chepstow (Wye Valley Junction); 6 January 1964 *(gds)*, Monmouth (Troy)–Tidenham Quarry.

*REMAINS* : Tintern station (SO 537007) and adjacent trackbed.

St. Briavels station (SO 537051). The route can be traced for much of the way up the valley and is most clearly seen between SO 527035 and the river bridge at SO 536098. The stone approaches of the river bridge near Monmouth (SO 514120) are intact but the steel span has been removed. The route can be followed from here to the site of Monmouth (Troy) station.

USES : Much of the trackbed is now privately-owned. However two stretches, one near Tintern station and the other running from Whitebrook (SO 538068) to Lower Redbrook (SO 536098), have been bought by the Gwent County Council and incorporated into the Wye Valley Walk. Tintern station and signalbox have also been purchased by the Gwent County Council and restored to their original conditions. The station building now incorporates a museum, part of which is devoted to the history of the branch. The remainder of the station site is laid out as a picnic area.

## PONTYPOOL AND ABERGAVENNY

Geography and the interplay of 19th century railway politics ensured Pontypool and Abergavenny important positions in the South Wales railway scene. The economic wheel has now come full circle. Little coal is exported from South Wales, and coal's markets are once again predominantly English. But the economic and political climates are totally different from a century ago, and the two stiffly-graded lines to Pontypool and Abergavenny from the west have given way to the longer main line through Newport. The important locomotive depots in these towns once provided the bulk of local employment. These are now only memories, as are journeys over the swaying vertiginous Crumlin viaduct, and up the precipitous Clydach gorge.

ABERGAVENNY (BRECON JUNCTION)–MERTHYR (RHYDYCAR JUNCTION)
24 miles
*Merthyr, Tredegar & Abergavenny Railway* (Abergavenny–Brynmawr)
*London & North Western Railway*—Jointly with *Rhymney Railway* and
*Brecon & Merthyr Railway* over two sections (Brynmawr–Merthyr (Rhydycar Junction)).
ACTS : 1 August 1859 (Merthyr, Tredegar & Abergavenny); 7 August 1862 (Lease to London & North Western Railway); 15 July 1867 (London & North Western Railway and Rhymney Railway (Joint)); 19 July 1875 (London & North Western and Brecon & Merthyr (Joint)).

*OPENED* : 29 September 1862 *(pass and gds)*, Abergavenny
(Brecon Junction)–Brynmawr; 1 March 1864 *(pass and gds)*,
Brynmawr–Nantybwch; 5 September 1871 *(pass and gds)*,
Nantybwch–Rhymney Bridge; 1 January 1873 *(pass and gds)*,
Rhymney Bridge–Dowlais (Ivor Junction); 1 June 1879 *(pass
and gds)*, Penywern Junction–Morlais Junction. The section
from Morlais Junction to Rhydycar Junction was joint with the
Brecon & Merthyr Tydfil Junction Railway and originally
opened 1 August 1868 (see Chapter 2).
*CLOSED* : 4 May 1885 *(pass)*, Penywern Junction–Ivor Junction.
22 November 1954 *(gds — through services)*, Abergavenny Junction–Morlais Junction, Penywern Junction–Ivor Junction. 6
January 1958 *(pass — through services)*, Abergavenny Junction–
Morlais Junction. Sections remained open after this date, their
closures were as follows: —
2 November 1959 *(gds)*, Nantybwch–Beaufort Brick Sidings;
13 June 1960 *(gds)*, 23 September 1963 *(min)*, Rhymney
Bridge–Nantybwch; 13 June 1960 *(pass)* Nantybwch *(Sirhowy
Valley service)*; 30 April 1962 *(pass)*, Brynmawr *(Newport service)*.
4 April 1971 *(gds)*, Abergavenny Junction–Brecon Road
Goods. For closures between Morlais Junction and Rhydycar
Junction, see Chapter 2.
*REMAINS* : At Abergavenny the red sandstone abutments and
sections of the approach embankments of the river bridge can
be seen at SO 292139; of note are the names of engineer and
contractor carved on each abutment. The station at Govilon is
remarkably intact. It is the only one that survives. Its single-
storey red sandstone buildings are on the down platform; level-
crossing gates still survive on the nearby road. Outstanding
views of the line can be seen when travelling along the A465.
Of special note is the shelf at SO 218124. The line is best
viewed from above, from the minor road at the above map
reference. At SO 197121, alongside the A465 just east of the
roundabout, the line reappears above the level of the road.
Little of the station area exists at Brynmawr, except the bridge
at SO 195116. The trackbed reappears at SO 187116 (note
bridge remains), running westwards towards Beaufort
station, the site of which has been obliterated by the re-
alignment of the junction of the A4047 and B4560 at SO
168117. The stretch finishes near SO 168117 as a trackbed
heading towards the A465. Between here and Dowlais Top the
A465 is laid on the railway, except near Nantybwch. Here, just
before the roundabout for Tredegar, a graceful nine-arch
limestone viaduct can be seen to the north at SO 133109.
Trackbed can be traced near the site of Penywern Junction,

where the line passed beneath the A465. The section Penywern Junction–Ivor Junction is completely buried beneath this road. North of the A465 the cutting can be seen emerging from beneath the road embankment. At SO 063092 is the southern portal of Morlais tunnel; the inscription is noteworthy. (Access to the northern portal is difficult.) The final remains of this line are two brick ventilating shafts for this tunnel alongside the road running to Pant station; a good viewing point would be SO 060095. The section from Morlais Junction to Merthyr has been described in the Ponsticill–Merthyr section of Chapter 2.

*USES* : Light industry is beginning to develop over the railway at Brynmawr. However, the principal use has been for the A465, Heads of the Valleys trunk road. Approximately 6½ miles have been taken. At Pantyscallog land has been used for a housing development.

BRYNMAWR–ABERSYCHAN & TALYWAIN                         8¼ miles
*London & North Western Railway.*
*ACT* : 16 July 1866 (Brynmawr & Blaenavon Railway, leased immediately to the London & North Western Railway).
*OPENED* : 1 November 1869 *(gds)*, 1 January 1870 *(pass)*, Brynmawr–Blaenavon; 1877 *(gds)* Blaenavon–Abersychan & Talywain. 13 July 1912 *(pass—worked by GWR)*, Brynmawr–Abersychan & Talywain.
*CLOSED* : 5 May 1941 *(pass)*, Brynmawr–Abersychan & Talywain; 23 June 1954 *(gds)* Brynmawr–Blaenavon Furnace Siding. 3 May 1980 (min), Waenavon–Abersychan & Talywain. (This section relaid March 1972 by and for the NCB).
*REMAINS* : Overbridge at SO 196116. Abersychan & Talywain buildings. Garndiffaith viaduct at SO 263043.
*USES* : Part of the trackbed at the northern end of the branch is being developed as an industrial estate. Near Big Pit mining museum (SO 235095) track in situ for Pontypool & Blaenavon Railway.

BEAUFORT (EBBW VALE JUNCTION)–EBBW VALE (HIGH LEVEL)
                                                      1¼ miles
*London & North Western Railway*
*ACT* : 5 July 1865
*OPENED* : 1 September 1867
*CLOSED* : 1 February 1951 *(pass)*; 2 November 1959 *(gds and min)*.
*REMAINS* : The only visible reminder of this branch is a short section of trackbed running south for a little distance from a point on the A4047 Beaufort–Brynmawr Road at SO 161115.

*USES* : The site of Ebbw Vale (HL) is now a multi-storey car park. Ebbw Vale leisure centre straddles the line about a ¼-mile north of the old terminus.

RHYMNEY BRIDGE—RHYMNEY                                                    1½ miles
*London & North Western Railway and Rhymney Railway Joint*
*ACT* : 15 July 1867
*OPENED* : 5 September 1871 *(pass and gds)*
*CLOSED* : 21 September 1953 *(pass and gds)* 23 September 1963 *(min)*
*REMAINS* : Little remains of this branch south of SO 107087, to the extant Rhymney station. Rhymney Bridge station site lies buried beneath the roundabout on the Heads of the Valleys road, although the station house survives nearby.
*USES* : Road improvements at the site of Rhymney Bridge station, and towards Rhymney.

BRYNMAWR—NANTYGLO                                                        1½ miles
*Brynmawr & Western Valleys Railway* (later *London & North Western Railway* and *Great Western Railway Joint*)
*ACTS* : 13 July 1899; 3 July 1902 (vested jointly in London & North Western Railway and Great Western Railway)
*OPENED* : 12 July 1905 *(gds)*, 28 May 1906 *(pass)*
*CLOSED* : 30 April 1962 *(pass)*, 4 December 1963 *(gds and min)*.
*REMAINS* : Only a short length of trackbed curving away from a point west of the junction with Abergavenny—Merthyr line can be traced. The only structure is an overbridge at SO 186110. It is built of blue brick and, interestingly, the roadway is cobbled.
*USES* : South of the overbridge to beyond Nantyglo, reclamation and amenity uses have removed all traces of the railway.

PONTYPOOL—NEATH                                                  35 miles 19 chains
*Newport, Abergavenny & Hereford Railway (Taff Vale Extension); Aberdare Valley Railway; Vale of Neath Railway.*
*ACTS* : 3 August 1846 (Vale of Neath Railway); 9 July 1847 (Newport, Abergavenny & Hereford Railway (Taff Vale extension)); 2 July 1855 (Aberdare Valley Railway).
*OPENED* :
*THROUGH LINE* : 11 January 1858 *(pass)*, Pontypool Road–Quakers Yard (Low level); 5 October 1864 *(pass)*, Quakers Yard Junction–Neath; 24 September 1851 *(pass)*, Aberdare (High Level)–Glyn Neath. 20 August 1855 *(gds)*, Pontypool Road–Crumlin Junction; 1 June 1857 *(gds)*, Crumlin Junction–Tredegar Junction (Pontllanfraith); 11 January 1858 *(gds)*, Tredegar Junction (Pontllanfraith)–Quakers Yard (Low

Level); 18 April 1864 *(gds)*, Quakers Yard Junction–Middle Duffryn Junction; November 1856 *(gds)*, Middle Duffryn Junction–Aberdare (Canal Head); June 1853 *(gds)*, Aberdare (Canal Head)–Aberdare (High Level); 24 September 1851 *(gds)*, Aberdare (High Level)–Neath; 24 August 1863 *(gds)*, Neath & Brecon Junction–Neath Junction.

*BRANCHES* : 20 October 1855 *(gds)*, Crumlin Junction–Llanhilleth Junction; 28 December 1863 *(gds)*, Maesycwmmer Junction–Fleur-de-Lis Junction; 13 November 1893 *(gds)*, Hengoed (High Level)–Ystrad Mynach North Junction, 30 December 1893 *(gds)*, Bird in Hand West Junction–Tredegar Junction (Pontllanfraith (High Level)).

*CLOSED* :

*THROUGH LINE* : 15 June 1964 *(pass)*, Pontypool Road–Neath. 15 June 1964 *(gds)*, Pontypool Road South Junction–Trosnant West Junction, Hafodyrnys West–Sirhowy Junction (excluding Penar Junction), Maesycwmmer Junction–Penallta Junction, Ocean & Taff Merthyr Collieries–Crescelly Crossing, Quakers Yard (East) Junction–Quakers Yard (Low Level Junction. 1 March 1965 *(gds)*, Crescelly crossing–Mountain Ash. 6 November 1967 *(gds)* Sirhowy Junction–Maesycwmmer Junction. 2 October 1967 *(gds and min)*, Glyn Neath–Hirwaun Pond. 4 October 1965 *(gds)*, Resolven–Aberpergwm. 21 March 1966 *(gds)*, Neath–Resolven. 15 August 1966 *(min & gds)*, Neath West Junction–Neath Junction. 4 March 1986 *(min)*, Neath & Brecon Junction–Aberpergwm. 1 April 1979 *(min)*, Trosnant West Junction–Hafodyrynys.

*BRANCHES* : 13 June 1960 *(gds)*, Bird-in-Hand West Junction–Tredegar Junction (Pontllanfraith (High Level)). 15 June 1964 *(gds)*, Hengoed (High Level)–Ystrad Mynach North. 17 May 1964 *(gds)*, Crumlin Junction–Llanhilleth Junction. 6 November 1967 *(gds)*, Maesycwmmer Junction–Fleur-de-Lis Junction. 5 April 1971 *(min)*, Dowlais (Cae Harris)–Dowlais (Furnace Top). 3 October 1983 *(min)*, Cwmbargoed–Dowlais (Furnace Top.)

*RE-OPENED* : 6 November 1967 *(min)*, Penar Junction–Bird-in-Hand (Pontllanfraith (Low Level)). See also Chapter 5, Risca Junction–Tredegar.

*FINAL CLOSURE* : 2 May 1970 *(min)*, Penar Junction–Bird-in-Hand (Pontllanfraith (Low Level)).

*REMAINS* : Trackbed can be followed, with varying degrees of difficulty for much of the route. A most impressive section is the site of the multi-level combined scissors and triangular formation formed by Bird-in-Hand, Sirhowy and Tredegar

(Lower) junctions at ST 176953. Equally impressive is the Glyn Neath Incline, which can be traced from SN 880061 to SN 910076. The four tunnels can be traced, Glyn at ST 227989, Bryn at ST 170950, Quakers Yard at ST 073968, and Pencaedrain at SN 918076, although access to the latter two is difficult. Two stone viaducts remain, Hengoed at ST 155949, and an unnamed one at SN 890064. The abutments of Crumlin viaduct still stand at ST 214987, and on the opposite side of the valley. Station sites have been reduced to overgrown platforms only, with the exception of Mountain Ash (Cardiff Road), ST 048993, and Hirwaun SN 961059. Abutments of the bridge across the A4059 remain at ST 063975. A typical GWR steel footbridge stands at the site of Quakers Yard (HL) station; it is the only access to the still open Low Level station on the Cardiff–Merthyr line. Track in situ Neath & Brecon Junction to Aberpergwm.

*USES*: Pontypool–Hafodyrynys is now beneath a new road (A472). Short lengths at Penar Junction, Penalltau Junction–Ocean & Taff Merthyr Collieries, Abercwmboi-Hirwaun (Rhigos), still in use as colliery branches by BR (WR). Road-widening schemes have claimed the trackbed at ST 221987, ST 177957 (Pontllanfraith LL station) and ST 094969.

QUAKERS YARD–MERTHYR (JOINT LINE JUNCTION)  5 miles 75 chains
*Great Western Railway & Rhymney Railway Joint*
*ACT*: 18 August 1882
*OPENED*: 1 April 1886 *(pass and gds)*
*CLOSED*: 3 February 1951 *(pass)*, Quakers Yard–Merthyr (Rhydycar Junction), Quakers Yard–Aberfan *(gds)*. 1 November 1954 *(gds)*, Aberfan–Abercanaid. 9 May 1960 *(gds)*, Abercanaid–Merthyr (Joint Line Junction).
*REMAINS*: The eastern abutments of the viaduct crossing the Taff valley stand immediately north of Quakers Yard station on the Taff valley line (ST 084967). The branch viaduct was the second abutment, the first one carried the Pontypool to Neath line across the valley.
*USES*: The trackbed has largely been used for the northern extension of the A470 Cardiff to Merthyr road.

GELLI TARW JUNCTION–MERTHYR (MARDY JUNCTION)
6 miles 23 chains
*Vale of Neath Railway*
*ACT*: 3 August 1846
*OPENED*: 2 November 1853 *(pass and gds)*
*CLOSED*: 31 December 1962 *(Pass and gds)*

REMAINS : The trackbed can be traced for much of the way from Gelli Tarw Junction to the south-west entrance of Merthyr tunnel. The high embankment running across the Taff valley from the north-east tunnel entrance remains intact.

USES : A housing development occupies the line at Abernant (SO 015035)

### CWMAMAN & DARE VALLEY BRANCHES

Aggregate mileage 9 miles 34 chains

*Vale of Neath Railway, Dare Valley Railway* (later *Taff Vale Railway*)

ACTS : 3 August 1846 (Vale of Neath Railway), 21 July 1863 (Dare Valley Railway)

OPENED : 7 November 1854 *(gds)*, Gelli Tarw Juntion–Dare Junction–Nantymelin Colliery. 2 November 1856 *(gds)*, Dare Junction–Cwmaman Colliery. 1 June 1857 *(gds)*, Nantymelin Colliery–Bwllfa Dare Colliery. 1866 *(gds)*, Dare Valley Junction–Bwllfa Dare Colliery. 1906 *(pass)*, Gelli Tarw Junction–Cwmaman Colliery.

CLOSED : 22 September 1924 *(pass)*, Gelli Tarw Junction-Cwmaman Colliery. 1 September 1939 *(gds)*, Gelli Tarw Junction–Dare Junction–Nantymelin Colliery.

REMAINS : The trackbed can be traced from the river crossing at SN 982049 to where it crossed the A4059; it is most easily seen at SN 986040, running through a cemetery. The line can then be traced from where it crosses the B4277 at SN 999023, to Cwmaman.

USES : The upper reaches of both the GWR and TVR branches have now been landscaped and form part of the Dare Valley Country Park. The lower part of the TVR branch is now a footpath (SN 999026). Children's parks occupy two sections of the line in Cwmaman, the one at ST 002995 marking the point beyond which no further trace can be found.

### PONTYPOOL (CRANE STREET)–BLAENAVON (LOW LEVEL)    5½ miles

*Monmouthshire Railway*

ACT : 31 July 1845

OPENED : 2 October 1854 *(pass and gds)*

CLOSED : 30 April 1962 *(pass)*, Pontypool (Crane Street)–Blaenavon (Low Level). 7 March 1960 *(gds)*, Snatchwood Sidings–Blaenavon (Low Level). May 1962 *(gds)*, Pontypool (Crane Street) (exclusive)–Snatchwood Sidings. 3 October 1966 *(gds)*, Pontypool (Crane Street). 3 May 1980 *(min)*, Pontypool (Crane Street)–Trevethin Junction.

REMAINS : The trackbed can be followed for most of the way from the site of Trevethin Junction to just south of the site of

*Plates 29 and 30.* Memories. *Above:* Cadoxton station on the Barry Railway, about 1905–1910, very different from today's remnant. No 94 'J' class and No 58 'B1' class on left. The station building on the right burnt down in 1911. *Below:* Aberdare locomotive shed about 1895–9. (*Welsh Industrial & Maritime Museum*)

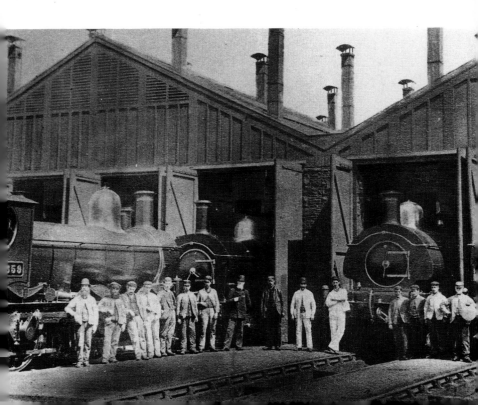

Plates *31 and 32*. Where steam survives. *Above*: The bay platform at Aberystwyth, which once held Carmarthen trains, is now the terminus of British Rail's only remaining fully steam-operated line, the narrow gauge Vale of Rheidol. *Below*: Preservation at Bronwydd Arms, on the Carmarthen–Aberystwyth line, operated by the Gwili Railway Company. (*J.H.R. Page*)

Blaenavon (LL). No engineering features of note remain.

*USES*: Road-widening or deviation have claimed sites near Trevethin Junction and Cwmffrwd. In Blaenavon the station area (SO 253085) has been redeveloped as a housing estate.

#### CWMFRWDOER & CWMNANTDDU BRANCHES
Aggregate mileage 3 miles 24 chains

*Monmouthshire Railway*
*ACT*: 31 July 1845
*OPENED*: 1870 *(min only)*
*CLOSED*: 7 April 1969 *(min)*
*REMAINS*: Branches Fork Junction can still be found at SO 266017 alongside the road in the village of Cwmnantddu. Of the Cwmfrwdoer branch its steep trackbed can be traced to SO 255006, beyond where land reclamation has obliterated every trace. Even less remains of the steeper companion branch, as much of it has been landscaped.

#### TREVETHIN JUNCTION–ABERSYCHAN & TALYWAIN   5 miles 60 chains
*Monmouthshire Railway; London & North Western Railway*
*ACTS*: 16 July 1874 (One Act from each company on the same day).
*OPENED*: 18 September 1879 *(gds)*, 13 July 1912 *(pass)*, Trevethin Junction–Abersychan & Talywain.
*CLOSED*: 5 May 1941 *(pass)*, 23 August 1965 *(gds)*, 3 May 1980 *(min)*, Trevethin Junction–Abersychan & Talywain.
*REMAINS*: Trackbed and earthworks throughout.

#### DOWLAIS RAILWAY
1 mile 68 chains
(Passenger section only)

*Dowlais Iron Company*
*ACT*: 28 July 1849
*OPENED*: 21 August 1851 *(pass and gds)*
*CLOSED*: 1854 *(pass)*. 1876 *(public goods traffic)*. October 1930 *(private goods to steelworks)*.
*REMAINS*: SO 055054 to SO 059061 the original incline, now landscaped and terraced. SO 055054 and SO 054053 bridge abutments over minor road and Cardiff–Merthyr Road. SO 054056 line of loop from incline to Vale of Neath Railway sidings.
*USES*: The landscaped and terraced incline has been grassed over and now serves as a recreational area for local children.

# NEWPORT

Newport, in its commanding position in the south-east corner of Wales, was always assured of a dominant position in the railway structure of the Principality. This position was secured by the evolution of both sea and land exits from the industrial hinterland, and as the former declined the latter grew. The importance that Newport had in the GWR structure was reflected in the establishment of the Newport Division, with powers over that company's Welsh affairs as far as Tondu and Aberdare. One of its main depots (Ebbw Junction) was situated to the west of the town. The site is now a housing estate. In the lifetime of the Great Western, and long after, it was one of the principal depots in South Wales, housing over one hundred locomotives.

When referring to Newport, one cannot omit the once famous 'Park Mile', where the traffic from the Western Valleys ran through the estate of Lord Tredegar. From 1805 until 1922, when the GWR bought-out the family interest in what was now a section no less than six tracks wide, tolls were extracted on every ton of minerals that passed.

NEWPORT (MILL STREET)–PONTYPOOL (CRANE STREET)          8 miles
*Monmouthshire Railway (Newport & Pontypool Railway)*
*ACT*: 31 July 1845
*OPENED*: 1 July 1852 *(pass and gds)*, Pontypool (Crane Street)–
    Newport (Marshes Turnpike Gate). 9 March 1853 *(pass and gds)*, Newport (Marshes Turnpike Gate)–Newport (Mill Street). NOTE: Cwmbran Junction was brought into operation in April 1878 on the opening of the loop to the Pontypool, Caerleon & Newport Railway at Llantarnum Junction.
*CLOSED*: 11 March 1880 *(pass)*, Newport (Mill Street)–
    Cwmbran Junction. 30 April 1962 *(pass)*, Pontypool (Crane Street)–Cwmbran Junction–Llantarnum Junction. 27 October 1963 *(gds)*, Oakfield Sidings–Crindau Sidings. 28 November 1966 *(gds)*, Crindau Sidings–Mill Street. 7 March 1967 *(gds)*, Cwmbran Junction–Oakfield Sidings. 3 May 1980 *(min)*, Pontypool (Crane St)–Cwmbran Junction–Llantarnum Junction.
*REMAINS*: ST 309892, from here running north is the embankment that once led to the bridge crossing Shaftesbury Street. ST 313900, above the portals of the M4 tunnels, a shelf can be seen running northwards. At ST 302920 a bridge carries the A4042 over a deep cutting. North of Cwmbran Junction sections of trackbed still in situ to Pontypool (Crane Street).

Bridges and viaduct at SO 283005 and SO 288003. Station buildings at Panteg & Griffithstown ST 295989.

*USES* : South of ST 309892 the site of Mill Street station has been excavated for the road complex passing beneath the South Wales main line. Much of the section between ST 302920 and ST 292950 has been used for roadworks.

NEWPORT STREET AND DOCK BRANCHES

Aggregate Mileage 2¾ miles

*Monmouthshire Railway; Pontypridd, Caerphilly & Newport Railway* (later *Alexandra (Newport & South Wales) Dock & Railway*).

*ACTS* : 31 July 1845 (Monmouthshire Railway), 2 August 1883 (Pontypridd, Caerphilly & Newport Railway).

*OPENED* : May 1855 *(pass and gds)*, Courtybella Junction–Dock Street. May 1855 *(gds)*, Courtybella Junction–Tredegar Wharf, Pillbank Junction–Dock Street, Dock Street–Mill Street, Llanarth Street Junction–Salutation Junction. April 1886 *(gds)*, Park Junction–Mendalgief East Junction.

*CLOSED* : 11 March 1880 *(pass)*, Courtybella Junction–Dock Street. 9 December 1907 *(gds)*, Courtybella Junction–Dock Street, Salutation Junction–Llanarth Street Junction. 3 September 1959 *(gds)*, Park Junction–Mendalgief East Junction. 28 November 1966 *(gds)*, Mill Street–Dock Street. 2 September 1979 *(min)*, Maesglas Junction–Mentalgief East Junction. 1981 *(min)*, Park Junction–Courtybella Junction.

*REMAINS* : Few traces of the ADR lines remain. They are the bridge carrying their line across the road near Bassaleg Junction (ST 282872), and bridge abutments carrying the dock branch across the main line at ST 303864, and also further east at ST 310862.

*USES* : All the closed street lines have been incorporated into roads or car parks. From Courtybella Junction (ST 309871) to Salutation Junction (ST 314874) the route exists as a sunken road on the south side of the A48. Outside the T&GWU offices (ST 314874) the line divided. The courses of Ebenezer Terrace (better known as Kingsway) and George Street were dictated by these lines. From Llanarth Street Junction (ST 314880) to Mill Street the trackbed has been used for the same roadworks mentioned in the previous section. Running south-east from this junction, and in the same direction from Pillbank Junction (ST 314869) car parks now occupy the trackbeds.

For details of Brecon & Merthyr lines in the Merthyr and Dowlais areas see Chapter 2.

BASSALEG–RHYMNEY (B&M)                                    22 miles
*Brecon & Merthyr Tydfil Junction Railway* (originally *Rumney Railway*)
ACT : 28 July 1863 (acquisition of Rumney Railway).
*OPENED* : 7 June 1865 *(pass and gds)*, Bassaleg–Pengam. 16 April 1866 *(pass and gds)*, Pengam–Rhymney (B&M).
*CLOSED* : 14 April 1930 *(pass and gds)*, New Tredegar–Rhymney (B&M). 31 December 1962 *(pass)*, Bedwas–New Tredegar. 31 December 1962 *(gds)*, Aberbargoed Junction–New Tredegar; Fleur-de-Lis Junction–Bedwas. 6 November 1967 *(gds)*, Pengam–Fleur-de-Lis Junction. 23 May 1982 *(min)*, Aberbargoed Junction–Pengam. 1 December 1986 *(min)*, Machen Quarry–Trethomas (Also Trethomas–Bedwas; NCB property from c.1969).
*REMAINS* : Much of the trackbed can be followed from Machen to Rhymney, the largest gap occurring north of New Tredegar, where a landslide in 1928 permanently severed the branch north of here. Station sites, none with any buildings, can be found at Pengam, Bargoed, Brithdir, New Tredegar and Rhymney (SO 121064). The latter is most interesting since the station closed in 1930. At Bedwas and Pengam, distinctive girder bridges can be found (ST 171894 and ST 157975 respectively). These are of Rumney Railway origin (ie the old tramway company), and bear cast-in inscriptions to this effect. From the bridge at ST 156986 the Rhymney branch trackbed is visible heading north.

The best remains of the Brecon & Merthyr Railway are to be found on the stretch from Machen to Newport. Of particular note is the stone viaduct (dating from 1826—again the old tramway) over the river Ebbw at ST 278872. Rhiwderin station (ST 259875) and Church Road station (ST 230884) are now privately-owned. The ruins of the B&M locomotive works stand at ST 217893.
*USES* : Remarkably little use has been made of this branch. Maesycwmmer station has succumbed to the inevitable road-widening. Pengam and New Tredegar station sites are play areas for local children.

BARGOED NORTH JUNCTION–PANT                              10¾ miles
*Brecon & Merthyr Tydfil Junction Railway (Pant-Deri); Rhymney Railway (Deri-Bargoed North Junction).*
*ACTS* : 6 August 1861 (both companies), 4 June 1864 (agreement with Rhymney Railway)
*OPENED* : 1 August 1867 *(pass and gds)*, Pant–Dowlais Top. 1 August 1868 *(pass and gds)*, Dowlais Top–Bargoed North

Junction. March 1864 *(gds)*, Bargoed North Junction–Deri Junction.

*CLOSED* : 31 December 1962 *(pass)*, Pant–Bargoed North Junction. 1 April 1963 *(gds)*, Pant Junction–Deri Junction. 23 August 1965 *(gds)*, Bargoed North Junction–Deri Junction.

*REMAINS* : Trackbed can be followed from Bargoed to Groes-fan, thence from Deri for most of the way to Pant. No station buildings remain, and only the sites of Deri station and Ogilvie Village Halt. Near here at SO 126026 is one of the distinctive small B&M overbridges—stone abutments, wooden-decked, with corrugated iron parapets, set in wooden frames.

*USES* : Between Groesfan and Deri land reclamation has covered the track. Fochriw station and surrounding area is now a council estate. The Heads of the Valley road cuts the line SO 086087. At SO 078084 a supermarket occupies the trackbed (at 1200ft above sea level). Cycle track Bargoed–Fochriw.

MACHEN–CAERPHILLY (EAST JUNCTION) 3¾ miles
*Brecon & Merthyr Tydfil Railway; Pontypridd, Caerphilly & Newport Railway* (later *Alexandra (Newport & South Wales) Dock & Railway)*
*ACTS* : 23 July 1863 (Brecon & Merthyr Tydfil Junction Railway), 1887 (Pontypridd, Caerphilly & Newport Railway).
*OPENED* : 1864 *(gds)*, 28 December 1887 *(pass)*, Machen Junction–Caerphilly East Junction. 14 September 1891 *(pass and gds)*, Machen Junction–Gwaunybara Junction (PC & N Line).
*CLOSED* : 17 September 1956 *(pass)*, 20 July 1964 *(gds)*, Machen Junction–Gwaunybara Junction (B&M Line). 20 November 1967 *(gds)*, Machen Junction–Caerphilly East Junction.
*REMAINS* : The trackbed of both the original branch and the later Machen Loop can be followed for most of the route. The outstanding remain is a 5-arch stone viaduct spanning the Rhymney at ST 202889, on the original section. From the road bridge at ST 190885 the stone piers of the bridge carrying the Machen Loop across the same river also remain. Similarly, looking east from the bridge at ST 177879 the site of Gwauny-bara junction is visible.
*USES* : Near Machen Junction private housing development and road-widening have obliterated the railway here.

PONTYPRIDD (PC&N JUNCTION)–PENRHOS JUNCTION 5 miles 12 chains
*Pontypridd, Caerphilly & Newport Railway* (later *Alexandra (Newport & South Wales) Dock & Railway)*.
*ACT* : 8 August 1878
*OPENED* : 7 July 1884 *(gds)*, 28 December 1887 *(pass)*.

*CLOSED* : 17 September 1956 *(pass)*, Pontypridd (PC&N Junction)–Penrhos Junction. 2 January 1967 *(gds)*, Penrhos Junction–Glyntaff. 31 July 1967 *(gds)*, Glyntaff–Pontypridd (PC&N Junction).

*REMAINS* : The line can be traced from Penrhos Junction, ST 136860, to above the A470 at ST 084896. Beyond this road the high embankment can be followed to the east bank of the river Taff.

*USES* : A short length at ST 083897 has been incorporated into the A470. The site near Glyntaff Halt (ST 086894) is now partially incorporated into the grounds of a local school. The line is used as a footpath through a housing estate at Rhydyfelin, ST 097885.

RISCA JUNCTION–NANTYBWCH                                    18 miles
*Monmouthshire Railway* (Risca–Nine Mile Point); *Sirhowy Railway* (Nine Mile Point–Nantybwch).

*ACTS* : 26 June 1802 (original Acts of both tramway companies). 31 July 1845 (Monmouthshire Railway). 25 May 1860 (Sirhowy Railway). 5 June 1865 (Sirhowy Railway extension to Nantybwch). 13 July 1876 (acquisition of Sirhowy Railway by London & North Western Railway).

*OPENED* : 1805 *(gds and min)*, 1822 *(pass)* — Original tramways. November 1855 *(gds)*, Risca Junction–Nine Mile Point. 19 June 1865 *(gds)*, Nine Mile Point–Sirhowy. 19 June 1865 *(pass)*, Risca Junction–Sirhowy (extended to Newport 5 July 1865). 2 November 1868 *(pass and gds)*, Sirhowy–Nanybwch.

*CLOSED* : The original passenger service (horse-drawn) ceased between 1850 and 1855. 13 June 1960 *(pass)*, Risca Junction–Nantybwch. 4 November 1963 *(gds and min)*, Nantybwch–Sirhowy. 15 June 1964 *(gds)*, Bird-in-Hand (Pontllanfraith (Low Level))–Tredegar Junction Lower. 6 November 1967 *(gds)*, Sirhowy Junction–Tredegar Junction Lower. 30 April 1969 *(gds and min)*, Sirhowy–Tredegar Junction Lower.

*RE-OPENED* : 6 November 1967 *(min)*, Bird-in-Hand (Pontllanfraith (Low Level))–Tredegar Junction Lower. See also Chapter 4, Pontypool–Neath.

*FINAL CLOSURE* : 2 May 1970 *(min)*, Bird-in-Hand (Pontllanfraith (Low Level))–Risca Junction.

*REMAINS* : The trackbed can be followed almost entirely from half a mile west of Risca to Nantybwch, and the sites of most stations can be found, notable exceptions being Pontllanfraith and Sirhowy. ST 239906, at the junction of this branch and the western valley line, is a tall abutment of the old Monmouthshire viaduct (do not confuse with the remains of the later bridge a few yards north). Pontllanfraith, at ST 177956 the extensive site of Bird-in-Hand Junction is laid out for view, together with the crossing of the LNWR and GWR lines.

*USES* : Pontllanfraith, the area north of Bird-in-Hand Junction involved in road-widening.

ABERBEEG JUNCTION–NANTYGLO                6 miles 10 chains
*Monmouthshire Railway*
*ACT* : 3 June 1792 (Monmouthshire Canal Company). 31 July 1845 (Monmouthshire Railway Company—conversion of tramways).
*OPENED* : 1824 (original tramroad). May 1855 *(pass & gds)*, Aberbeeg Junction–Nantyglo Gate.
*CLOSED* : 30 April 1962 *(pass)*, Aberbeeg Junction–Nantyglo. 30 April 1962 *(gds)*, Nantyglo. 7 April 1969 *(gds)*, Aberbeeg Junction–Abertillery. 29 October 1973 *(min)*, Coalbrookvale–Nantyglo. 5 July 1976 *(min)*, Rose Heyworth Colliery–Coalbrookvale. 5 April 1986 *(min)*, Aberbeeg Junction–Rose Heyworth.
*REMAINS* : Track in situ Aberbeeg Junction–Six Bells Colliery.
*USES* : From Six Bells northwards to Nantyglo the trackbed has been, or will shortly be, used for road-works.

CWMTILLERY BRANCH                         75 chains
*Monmouthshire Railway.*
*ACT* :
*OPENED* : November 1858 *(min & gds)*, Cwmtillery Branch Junction–Cwmtillery.
*CLOSED* : 1 April 1963 *(min)*, Cwmtillery Branch Junction–Cwmtillery Colliery.
*REMAINS* : Overbridge at SO 217043.
*USES* : Northwards from SO 217043 light industry and a public park.

EBBW VALE (DUFFRYN SIDINGS)–BEAUFORT      2 miles 27 chains
*Monmouthshire Railway.*
*ACT* : 3 June 1792 (Monmouthshire Canal Company). 31 July 1845 (Monmouthshire Railway Company—conversion of tramways).
*OPENED* : 1798 (original tramroad). May 1855 *(pass & gds)*. The alignment of this section was altered as the steelworks expanded.
*CLOSED* : 30 April 1962 *(pass)*, 1 December 1969 *(gds)*, Ebbw Vale (Low Level)–Duffryn Sidings. 1939 *(min)*, Beaufort Iron Works. March 1962 *(min)*, Beaufort Iron Works–Beaufort Coal

Yard. 8 December 1969 *(min)*, Beaufort Coal Yard–Ebbw Vale
(Low Level). 15 June 1975 *(min)*, Ebbw Vale (Low Level)–
Ebbw Vale Sidings. October 1977 *(min)*, Ebbw Vale Sidings–
Duffryn Sidings.
*REMAINS* : Trackbed can be traced alongside the Ebbw Vale
steelworks.
*USES*: Alongside the Ebbw Vale steelworks sections of trackbed
now used as a car park.

CWMCARN BRANCH                                           72 chains
*Great Western Railway.*
*ACT* : 16 August 1909.
*OPENED* : April 1911 *(min & gds)*, Cwmcarn Branch Junction–
Cwmcarn Colliery.
*CLOSED* : 29 November 1978 *(min)*, Cwmcarn Branch Junction–
Cwmcarn Colliery.
*REMAINS* : Part of trackbed can be traced beyond junction.

OAKDALE COLLIERY–MARKHAM COLLIERY        2 miles 41 chains
*Halls Tramroad. Great Western Railway.*
*ACT* : None. Tramroad built circa 1805, leased by GWR 1877.
*OPENED* : 10 March 1886 *(min)*, Oakdale–Llanover Colliery
(conversion of Halls Tramroad). Opened progressively to
Markham Colliery up to October 1914 as new collieries were
sunk.
*CLOSED* : 31 December 1979 *(min)*, Oakdale Colliery–Markham
Colliery.
*REMAINS* : Trackbed can be traced.

# CARDIFF AND BARRY

To the casual observer Cardiff maintains a busy railway system.
It is only to those who knew the City in the years gone by that the
decline is noticeable. The last load of export coal departed many
years ago. Two docks only remain open, and their only rail
connection is from the east off the South Wales main line. Apart
from Inter-City services, Cardiff generates a substantial, though
heavily subsidised, commuter traffic from the hinterland and the
Barry and Penarth areas. Unhappily, stopping passenger traffic
along the main line, to such places at St Fagans, Marshfield and
stations further afield, is now a rapidly-fading memory.

Once Cardiff boasted numerous locomotive sheds, including
Cardiff (Canton) — GWR, Cathays and Radyr — TVR, and East
Dock — RR, together with the TVR locomotive works. Only
Cardiff (Canton) now remains, rebuilt as the main diesel depot

for the area. Interestingly, parts of the two steam sheds built on the same site are still visible, incorporated into the modern structure. Outside Cardiff, of the sheds that once existed, within the area covered by this chapter (about twenty, depending upon the precise time period) all are now closed and many demolished. Only a few remain in railway use as stabling points.

BLAENRHONDDA BRANCH                                            1 ½ miles
*Rhondda & Hirwaun Junction Railway* (later *Taff Vale Railway*)
*ACTS* : 12 August 1867; 17 June 1878 (leased to Taff Vale Railway)
*OPENED* : 17 June 1878 *(min)*
*REMAINS* : From the point where the line passes beneath the R&SB line at SS 929992 the line can be traced to the site of Blaenrhondda colliery. The low northern abutment of the bridge over the Rhondda Fawr can be found at SS 929991.
*USES* : A factory occupies the site of the junction with the Taff Vale Railway. A bungalow has been built across the line immediately south of the R&SB embankment.

PWLLYRHEBOG–CLYDACH VALE COLLIERY           2 miles 5 chains
*Taff Vale Railway*
*ACT* : 17 August 1857, (Pwllyrhebog Branch Junction–Pwllyrhebog). The section from Pwllyrhebog to Clydach Vale Colliery was built privately and acquired by the Taff Vale Railway in 1896.
*OPENED* : 1863 *(gds and min)*, Pwllyrhebog Branch Junction–Pwyllyrhebog. 1889 Pwllyrhebog–Clydach Vale Colliery.
*CLOSED* : 1 July 1951
*REMAINS* : Stone bridge abutments (SS 993927). The incline can be followed up the hill; it is partially landscaped, and is best viewed from SS 988927. The alignment can be followed to SS 981928.
*USES* : West of SS 981928 land reclamation has obliterated all traces.

NELSON BRANCH                                     5 miles 22 chains
                                    (Original branch 3 miles 29 chains)
*Taff Vale Railway*
*ACTS* : 21 June 1836 (Original branch, Stormstown Junction–Nelson). 21 July 1879 (Pont-Shon-Norton Junction–Ynysydwr Junction).
*OPENED* : 1841 *(gds and min)*, Stormstown Junction–Nelson. (Date unknown–deviation avoiding incline). 1887 *(gds and min)*, Pont-Shon-Norton Junction–Cilfynydd. 1900 *(gds and*

*min)*, Cilfynydd–Ynysydwr Junction. 1 June 1900 *(pass)*, Pont-Shon-Norton Junction–Nelson.

*CLOSED* : (Date unknown–incline). 12 September 1932 *(pass)* Pont-Shon-Norton Junction–Nelson. 1939 *(gds)* Albion Colliery (Cilfynydd)–Nelson. Remainder 1949.

*REMAINS* : The original incline. This is most clearly seen by turning off the A470 at ST 089949 and driving up the hill to the second hairpin bend. At this point the road crosses the track of the original branch, which can clearly be seen to right and left. An easy walk along the right-hand trackbed leads to the incline top (ST 084943). On returning from the site of the original track to the main road, the road turns sharply left, at this point (ST 090950) the road crosses a partially-filled cutting which carried the later deviation of the branch which avoided the incline. The road bridge and viaduct over the river at Pont-Shon-Norton Junction stand at ST 077912. Both are intact.

*USES* : ST 113954 (site of Nelson Station).—Cutting filled-in and now used as a bus station. Portions of the line from approximately ST 082912 to ST 087948, including the site of Travellers' Rest and Cilfyndd Stations, now used for A470 Cardiff–Merthyr Road.

BARRY ISLAND–BARRY PIER                                    43 chains
*Barry Railway*
*ACTS* : 7 August 1896
*OPENED* : 27 June 1899
*CLOSED* : 19 October 1971
*REMAINS* : ST 122668 tunnel beneath headland from Barry Island station.
*USES* : Station site now incorporated into a boat yard.

CADOXTON JUNCTION–TREHAFOD JUNCTION & BRANCHES
                                                   17 miles 12 chains
(AND TONTEG JUNCTION–TREFOREST JUNCTION)    14 miles 1 chain
*Barry Railway*
*ACT* : 14 August 1884
*OPENED* : 13 May 1889 *(gds and min)*, Cadoxton–Tynycaeau Junction. 18 July 1889 *(gds and min)*, Tynycaeau Junction–Trehafod Junction (and Tonteg Junction–Treforest Junction); Tynycaeau Junction–St. Fagans Junction; Drope Junction–Peterston East Junction. 16 March 1896 *(pass)*, Cadoxton–Trehafod Junction; Tynycaeau Junction–St. Fagans Junction. 10 July 1930 *(pass)*, Tonteg Junction–Treforest Junction.

*CLOSED* : 1 July 1925 *(gds)*, Tynycaeau Junction–St. Fagans Junction. 10 July 1930 *(pass)*, Tonteg Junction–Trehafod

Junction. 1943 (Up line), June 1951 (Down line) *(gds and min)*, Tonteg Junction–Pwllgwaen (near Trehafod). 4 July 1956 *(gds and min)*, Pwllgwaen–Trehafod Junction. 10 September 1962 *(pass)*, Cadoxton–Treforest Junction; Tynycaeau Junction–St. Fagans Junction. 1 March 1963 *(gds and min)*, Drope Junction–Peterston East Junction. 2 December 1963 *(gds and min)*, Cadoxton–Treforest Junction.

*REMAINS* : Nearest to Cadoxton, the first noteworthy remain is a fine brick overbridge at ST 130719. At ST 128733 stands Wenvoe station, the best-preserved example of Barry Railway station architecture. An airshaft of the Wenvoe tunnel can be seen on the left a few hundred yards from the roundabout at ST 122743, travelling along the Cardiff–Barry road (A4050). The sites of Creigiau and Efail Isaf stations remain, but no buildings. In the Taff valley, the impressive hillside shelves dropping to Trehafod and Treforest Junctions remain.

The site of Graig station can still be found at ST 069897, with the northern portal of Graig tunnel at the platform ends (no buildings remain). In the Rhondda valley the last mile to Trehafod Junction can be traced, as can the bridge abutments at ST 049910.

*USES* : A section of trackbed north of Wenvoe tunnel is now used as a motorway link road. The railway viaducts across the Ely valley have been replaced by road viaducts on the same sites. The site of Cadoxton Junction and adjacent sidings is now a housing estate. Wenvoe station is now a private house. In Pontypridd, the Post Office has erected offices immediately north of Graig station.

RHYMNEY BRANCH                                                    9½ miles
*Barry Railway*
*ACTS* : 7 August 1896 (Tynycaeau Junction–Penrhos Upper Junction), 25 July 1898 (Penrhos Lower Junction–Barry Junction (B&M)).
*OPENED* : 1 August 1901 *(gds and min)*, Tynycaeau Junction–Penrhos Upper Junction. 2 January 1905 *(gds and min)*, Penrhos Lower Junction–Barry Junction (B&M). 1924 *(pass)*, Penrhos Upper Junction–Tynycaeau Junction (summer time-table only). 1926 *(gds and min)*, Penrhos Lower Junction–Barry Junction (B&M).
*CLOSED* : 1935 *(pass)*, Penrhos Upper Junction–Tynycaeau Junction (at end of summer timetable). 17 June 1963 *(gds and min)*, Tynycaeau Junction–Walnut Tree West. 18 December 1967 *(min)*, Walnut Tree West–Penrhos Upper Junction.
*REMAINS* : A fine overbridge still stands on the A4119 at ST

115799, and much of the trackbed can still be traced. The remains of the once-famous viaducts at Taffs Well and Llanbradach can still be seen. The 'Taffs Well' from the Cardiff–Merthyr Road (A470) at ST 128827 and the 'Llanbradach' from the Caerphilly Hengoed Road (A469) at ST 149891. Penrhos Upper Junction site ST 126860 can be seen from the nearby overbridge.

*NOTE* : The only regular passenger services ran between the dates shown above. However, the line was regularly used for holiday excursion traffic from the Rhymney valley and surrounding area, to Barry Island. The first such excursion ran on 24 April 1905, and the last in 1964.

PENARTH–CADOXTON BRANCH                    4 miles 55 chains
*Cardiff, Penarth & Barry Junction Railway*
*ACT* : 6 August 1885. (26 August 1889 absorbed by the Taff Vale Railway).
*OPENED* : 1 December 1887 to Biglis Junction only, extended to Cadoxton 20 December 1888 *(gds)*. August 1889 *(pass)*.
*CLOSED* : 6 May 1968 *(pass)*. 7 October 1963 *(gds)*.
*REMAINS* : Much of the trackbed of this branch can be followed from Penarth Town station (ST 185715) to ST 146691. Unfortunately most of the bridges that once graced this line have been demolished. However, their style and proportions can be gauged from the small underbridge at ST 148688, which can be seen from the B4267.
*USES* : Penarth Station down platform is now used by an agricultural implements firm, the goods yard is now a housing estate. Lavernock Station goods shed now houses an electronics firm and the cutting near the site of Sully station has been used for horticultural purposes.

CORYTON–TREFOREST                              6¾ miles
*Cardiff Railway*
*ACT* : 6 August 1897
*OPENED* : 15 May 1909 *(gds)*, Treforest–Heath Junction. 1 March 1911 *(pass)*, Rhydyfelin–Heath Halt (Low Level).
*CLOSED* : 20 July 1931 *(pass and gds)*, Rhydyfelin–Coryton Halt.
*RE-OPENED* : 28 August 1951 *(min)*, Nantgarw Colliery–Coryton Halt.
*FINAL CLOSURE* : 16 June 1952 *(min)*, Nantgarw Colliery–Coryton Halt (on the same day a new connection was opened from the colliery to the ex-TVR line at Taffs Well. A small section of the ex-Cardiff Railway line was incorporated).

*REMAINS* : At ST 147809 is a road bridge immediately west of Coryton Halt. Looking west is a view of the cutting curving away northwards. At ST 120846 stands a lattice girder overbridge built askew to the road (the old Cardiff–Merthyr road). This bridge is actually on the short stretch of this line that linked the Nantgarw Colliery to Taffs Well. It is worth mentioning here for the fine workmanship in the stone abutments, the south-eastern one of which bears the inscribed date of 1907. At ST 088883 is the western abutment of the one-time bridge across the river Taff. This abutment and the tall embankment behind it curving northwards to the long defunct junction with the Taff Vale Railway can be seen to advantage whilst travelling northwards on the A470. Two minor over-bridges at ST 108868 and ST 109866.

*USES* : Approximately four miles of the line have now been buried beneath the A470 Cardiff–Merthyr trunk road.

ROATH BRANCH                         4 miles 76 chains
*Taff Vale Railway*
*ACT* : 6 August 1885
*OPENED* : 23 April 1888
*CLOSED* : 6 May 1968
*REMAINS* : The deep cutting near the junction is still extant. Prior to the construction of the Cardiff Inner Relief Road (Eastern Avenue) this cutting was approximately twice as long, (ST 163792). Only one bridge remains on the southern part of the branch at ST 199782.

*USES* : Much of the trackbed of the northern end of this branch has been incorporated into Eastern Avenue. The embankment carrying this road across the southern end of Roath Park (ST 185788) was originally the railway embankment.

EAST DOCK BRANCH                   1 mile 20 chains
*Rhymney Railway*
*ACT* : 2 July 1855.
*OPENED* : September 1857 *(gds)*, 31 March 1858 *(pass)*, to original Adam Street Station.
*CLOSED* : 3 January 1965 *(gds and min)*, Adam Street Goods–Stonefield Junction. 2 May 1966 *(gds and min)*, Queen Street North Junction–Adam Street Goods.
*REMAINS* : A few isolated sections of the embankment south of ST 194763 still remain, running into the dock area.
*USES* : Road improvements have obliterated the site of the Adam Street goods depot (originally the Rhymney Railway passenger terminus), the trackbed North West, together with

the adjacent Taff Vale Railway Queens Street Goods Yard, is now occupied by British Rail's sometime Welsh headquarters, Brunel House.

TYNDALL STREET BRANCH                                    45 chains
*London & North Western Railway*
*ACT* :
*OPENED* : 1875 *(gds only)*
*CLOSED* : 1 July 1933 to LMS traffic. The branch continued in use as a siding serving Tyndall Street goods depot until the widespread rail closures in the dock area.
*REMAINS* : Tyndall Street goods depot still stands, at ST 190759. It is disused and no longer rail-connected.

RIVERSIDE BRANCH                                         78 chains
*Great Western Railway*
*ACTS* : 6 August 1880, 5 August 1891
*OPENED* : 14 September 1882 *(gds)*. 2 April 1894 *(pass)*. Passenger traffic was of the Barry and Taff Vale Railways (not GWR until grouping).
*CLOSED* : 16 March 1964 *(pass)*, Cardiff (Clarence Road)–Cardiff (General). 16 March 1964 *(gds)*, Cardiff (Clarence Road)–Riverside North signalbox. 8 July 1968 *(gds)*, Riverside North signalbox–Cardiff (General).
*REMAINS* : Platforms 8 and 9 (now in use for parcels traffic only), at Cardiff Central *(formerly* General) station were the branch platforms.

ABER JUNCTION–SENGHENYDD                          3 miles 27 chains
*Rhymney Railway*
*ACT* : 25 July *1890*.
*OPENED* : 1 February 1894 *(pass & gds)*, Aber Junction–Senghenydd.
*CLOSED* : 15 June 1964 *(pass)*, Aber Junction–Senghenydd. 2 July 1962 *(gds)*, Abertridwr–Senghenydd. 1 March 1965 *(gds)*, Aber Junction–Abertridwr. 5 September 1977 *(min)*, Aber Junction–Windsor Colliery North Ground Frame.
*REMAINS* : Sections of trackbed can be traced north westwards from Aber Junction. Overbridge at ST 141879.

CAERPHILLY WEST JUNCTION–PENRHOS JUNCTION    1 mile 9 chains
& BEDDAU LOOP                                            20 chains
*Rhymney Railway*
*ACT* : 10 August 1857 (Penrhos Junction–Caerphilly)
*OPENED* : 1859 *(min)*, 25 July 1884 *(pass—used by PC&N only)*,

Caerphilly West Junction–Penrhos Junction. Date of opening
of Beddau Loop not known.
CLOSED: 1 May 1967 *(pass & gds)*, Caerphilly West Junction–
Penrhos Junction. 1 May 1967 *(min)*, Beddau Loop.
REMAINS : Trackbed of both lines can be traced. Site of level
crossing at ST 147865.

WALNUT TREE JUNCTION–ABER JUNCTION          3 miles 32 chains
*Rhymney Railway*
ACT : 2 July 1855
OPENED : 25 February 1858 *(gds)*, 31 March 1858 *(pass)*, Aber
Junction–Walnut Tree Junction.
CLOSED : 1 April 1871 *(pass)*, 21 June 1982 *(min)*, Aber
Junction–Walnut Tree Junction.
REMAINS : Trackbed. Skew bridge over A470 at ST 125835.
Overbridge at ST 141864. Rhymney Railway engine shed in
private use near Walnut Tree Junction.

PORTH (RHONDDA FACH JUNCTION NORTH)–MAERDY
                                             6 miles 38 chains
*Taff Vale Railway*
ACTS : 26 August 1846. 17 August 1857
OPENED : March 1849 *(min)*, Porth–Ynyshir. 1859 *(min)*,
Ynyshir–Ferndale. May 1877 *(min)*, (privately built line
completed from Ferndale to Maerdy). 1876 *(pass)*, Porth–
Ferndale. 18 June 1889 *(pass)*, Ferndale–Maerdy.
CLOSED : 1 March 1956 *(gds)*, 15 June 1964 *(pass)*, Porth–
Maerdy. 3 July 1986 *(min)*, Porth–Maerdy Colliery.
REMAINS : The track remains in situ pending a decision on
future use.
USES : None, but proposals are under review to reopen the line
for passenger use.

EIRW BRANCH                                       73 chains
*Taff Vale Railway*
ACT : 26 August 1846.
OPENED : 1854 *(min)*, Eirw Branch Junction–Cymmer and
other collieries.
CLOSED : November 1976 *(min)*, Eirw Branch Junction–Lewis
Merthyr Colliery.

RHONDDA CUTTING JUNCTION–NORTH CURVE JUNCTION     18 chains
*Taff Vale Railway*
ACT :
OPENED : October 1872 *(min & gds)*, Rhondda Cutting
Junction

–North Curve Junction.

*CLOSED* : 5 August 1968 *(min & gds)*, Rhondda Cutting Junction–North Curve Junction.

*REMAINS* : Short cutting.

NANTGARW COLLIERY BRANCH JUNCTION–NANTGARW COLLIERY
2 miles 30 chains

*Cardiff Railway. British Railways (Western Region)*

*ACT* : 6 August 1897 (Cardiff Railway).

*OPENED* : 16 June 1952 *(min)*, Nantgarw Colliery Branch Junction–Nantgarw Colliery. (Approximately 2 miles of this branch was ex Cardiff Railway opened 15 May 1909. For further details see p172 CORYTON–TREFOREST).

*CLOSED* : 11 April 1987 *(min)*, Nantgarw Colliery Branch Junction–Nantgarw Colliery.

*REMAINS* : Track still in situ. (See also pp 172/3).

*USES* : Temporarily in use for wagon storage.

STORMSTOWN JUNCTION–LLANWONNO COLLIERY   4 miles 67 chains
CLYDACH COURT JUNCTION–CLYDACH LOOP JUNCTION
1 mile 11 chains

*Taff Vale Railway*

*ACT* : 21 July 1873. 17 August 1894 (Clydach Court Junction–Clydach Loop Junction).

*OPENED* : 1886 *(min & gds)*, Ynysybwl Branch (Stormstown) Junction–Llanwonno Colliery. March 1890 *(pass)*, Ynysybwl Branch (Stormstown) Junction–Ynysbwl. 1900 *(gds & min)*, 1 November 1904 *(pass)*, Clydach Court Junction–Clydach Loop Junction–Ynysybwl.

*CLOSED* : 1 November 1904 *(pass)*, Ynysybwl Branch (Stormstown) Junction–Clydach Loop Junction. 28 July 1952 *(pass)*, 2 November 1959 *(gds)*, Clydach Court Junction–Ynysybwl. December 1938 *(min)*, Old Ynysybwl Halt–Llanwonno Colliery. Date not known: Clydach Court Junction–Clydach Loop Junction. Stormstown Junction–Lady Windsor Colliery (Ynysybwl) still open for mineral traffic but the closure of the colliery has been announced.

*REMAINS* : Trackbed beyond Ynysybwl, but difficult to trace.

ELY TIDAL HARBOUR BRANCH                    1 mile (approx)

*Penarth Dock, Harbour & Railway. (Originally called Ely Tidal Harbour & Railway).*

*ACT* : 21 August 1856 (Ely Co.) 27 July 1857 (Penarth Co.).

*OPENED* : August 1859 *(min & gds)*, as the termination of the Penarth Branch Junction (Radyr)–Ely Tidal Harbour line, from Grangetown Junction to wharves.

*CLOSED* : Not known. A short section to the site of the gas works and oil storage sidings is still in use.

*REMAINS* : None south of remaining section.

*USES* : Site incorporated into road-works in connection with the redevelopment of Cardiff dockland.


## LLANTRISANT AND BRIDGEND

The Vale of Glamorgan was served well by its railways, but has suffered the usual fate of regions between large conurbations—a total loss of facilities for local goods and passenger traffic. On the two lines that still cross the area, the South Wales main line, and the Vale of Glamorgan line from Barry to Bridgend, only one station (Bridgend) remains, when once there were eleven. If one includes all the branches in this area, some of which have been described in this chapter, stations and halts closed rise to 43. For that which remains the future appears secure. In fact a new branch has been built from the Vale of Glamorgan line to the Ford Motor Company's new factory near Bridgend.

CEFN JUNCTION–PORTHCAWL                                    7 miles
*Llynfi Valley Railway*
*ACT* : 7 August 1846
*OPENED* : 10 August 1861 *(gds)*, 1 August 1865 *(pass)*, Cefn Junction–Porthcawl. 13 November 1876 *(pass and gds)*, Pyle East Junction. 15 September 1946 *(pass and gds)*, Pyle West Junction–Heol y sheet Junction.
*CLOSED* : 9 September 1963 *(pass)*, Cefn Junction–Porthcawl. 1 February 1965 *(gds)*, Pyle East Junction–Porthcawl, Pyle West Junction–Heol y sheet Junction. 19 November 1973 *(gds)*, Cefn Junction–Pyle East Junction.
*REMAINS* : At Pyle the remains of the junction and approach line from Cefn are visible from the bridge at SS 828818. The branch ran under the nearby roundabout, and can be followed beyond it (to the west of the M4 approach road). The course of Pyle west loop can be seen at SS 825816. At Nottage, the tunnel still remains (SS 820780). Nothing of the railway remains in Porthcawl, but one reminder of the horse-drawn tramway can be seen; on the breakwater a short length of tramway track has been preserved *in situ*.
*USES* : At Pyle and Porthcawl road improvements have used the railway land.

WATERHALL JUNCTION–PYLE                              75 chains
*Cefn & Pyle Railway* (later *Port Talbot Railway & Dock Company*)
*ACT* : 7 August 1896 (Port Talbot railway acquisition)
*OPENED* : 19 December 1898
*CLOSED* :
*REMAINS* : None
*USES* : Working northwards from Pyle a garden centre, super-
market and council estate now occupy the land over which this
line once ran.


BRYNMENIN JUNCTION–BLAENGARW                   5 miles 74 chains
*Llynfi & Ogmore Railway*
*ACT* : 23 July 1866
*OPENED* : 25 October 1876 *(min and gds)*, 1 May 1902 *(pass)*,
Brynmenin Junction–Blaengarw.
*CLOSED* : 9 February 1953 *(pass)*, Brynmenin Junction–
Blaengarw. 2 July 1962 *(gds)*, Pontycymmer–Blaengarw. 19
July 1965 *(gds)*, Brynmenin Junction–Pontycymmer. 8 May
1986 *(min)*, Brynmenin Junction–Blaengarw.
*REMAINS* : The track remains in situ and the station sites are
still identifiable.


TONDU MIDDLE JUNCTION–NANTYMOEL              7 miles 18 chains
*Ogmore Valley Railway*
*ACT* : 13 July 1863
*OPENED* : 1 August 1865 *(pass and gds)*, Tondu Middle
Junction–Nantymoel.
*CLOSED* : 5 May 1958 *(pass)*, Tondu Middle Junction–
Nantymoel. 19 November 1962 *(gds)*, Ogmore Vale–Nanty-
moel. 23 November 1964 *(gds)*, Brynmenin Junction–Ogmore
Vale. 19 July 1965 *(gds)*, Tondu Middle Junction–Brynmenin
Junction. 21 October 1983 *(min)*, Caedu Crossing–Nantymoel.
16 July 1986 *(min)*, Tondu Middle Junction–Caedu Crossing.
*REMAINS* : The track remains in situ as far as Caedu Crossing,
beyond which the course of the line can be followed. Station
sites are still identifiable.


CARDIFF & OGMORE JUNCTION–LLANHARAN         8 miles 24 chains
*Cardiff & Ogmore Railway* (later *Llynfi & Ogmore Railway*)
*ACT* : 21 July 1873
*OPENED* : 2 October 1876 *(min only)*
*CLOSED* : 28 July 1938, Cardiff & Ogmore Junction–Bryncethin
Junction. 3 December 1962, Llanharan–Wern Tarw East
Ground Frame. 31 July 1967, Wern Tarw East Ground
Frame–Wern Tarw West Ground Frame. 9 March 1982 *(min)*,

Wern Tarw West Ground Frame–Bryncethin Junction.

*REMAINS* : The junction site remains at Blackmill and can be seen from across the valley at SS 928875. From SS 932864 the trackbed can be followed for most of the way to Llanharan. The piers of the viaduct at Blackmill stand at SS 934867.

*USES* : Two short sections either side of the viaduct have been absorbed in housing developments.

BLACK MILL–HENDREFORGAN                          3 miles 30 chains
*Llynfi & Ogmore Railway*
*ACT* : 28 June 1866
*OPENED* : 1 September 1875 *(pass and gds)*
*CLOSED* : 22 September 1930 *(pass)*. 27 March 1961 *(gds)*
*REMAINS* : The entire trackbed and bridges remain intact along the whole route from SS 933865 to SS 980875.

BRYNCETHIN JUNCTION–TYNYCOED JUNCTION            1 mile 77 chains
*Llynfi & Ogmore Railway*
*ACT* : 21 July 1873
*OPENED* : 1 May 1877 *(gds)*
*CLOSED* : 9 March 1982 *(min)*, Bryncethin Junction–Tynycoed Junction (and Ynysawdre Junction).
*REMAINS* : The most prominent feature is the bridge over the A4061 at SS 915842. Overbridges at SS 922840 and 932838.

LLANTRISANT–BLAENCLYDACH                         8 miles 75 chains
*Ely Valley Railway, Ely & Clydach Valley Railway*
*ACTS* : 13 July 1857 (Ely Valley Railway), 5 August 1873 (Ely & Clydach Valley Railway)
*OPENED* : 2 August 1860 *(gds)*, Llantrisant–Tonyrefail. December 1862 *(gds)*, Tonyrefail–Penygraig. 10 August 1878 *(gds)*, Penygraig–Blaenclydach. 1 May 1901 *(pass)*, Llantrisant–Penygraig.
*CLOSED* : 9 June 1958 *(pass)*, 12 October 1964 *(gds)*, Llantrisant–Penygraig. 3 April 1967 *(min)*, Coed Ely South Ground Frame–Blaenclydach. 2 April 1984 *(min)*, Mwyndy Junction–Coed Ely South Ground Frame.
*REMAINS* : Only the trackbed remains south of Coed Ely.
*USES* : The end of the branch has been lost beneath landscaping (see also Pwllyrhebog branch, Chapter 6). Tonyrefail–Penygraig used for a new road.

GELLIRHIADD JUNCTION–GILFACH GOCH                3¾ miles
*Ely Valley Railway, Ely Valley Extension Railway* (later *Llynfi & Ogmore Railway*)

*ACTS* : 13 July 1857 (Ely Valley Railway). 28 July 1863 (Ely Valley Extension Railway).

*OPENED* : 8 January 1862 *(gds)*, Gellirhiadd Junction–Gellirhiadd. 16 October 1864 *(gds)*, Gellirhiadd–Gilfach Goch, *(pass)* Hendreforgan–Gilfach Goch. (Passenger service worked from Blackmill–Gilfach Goch, with reversal at Hendreforgan.)

*CLOSED* : 22 September 1930 *(pass)*, Hendreforgan–Gilfach Goch. 5 June 1961 *(gds and min)*, Gellirhiadd Junction–Gilfach Goch.

*REMAINS* : The trackbed only remains near Gellirhiadd Junction (ST 008872), to the site of Gilfach Goch (SS 978888). The most noticeable feature of the line, the hillside shelf south of the station, can best be seen from SS 978877.

*USES* : A short length is used as a footpath, south of Gilfach Goch station. North of here all traces of the railway have been removed following landscaping.

LLANTRISANT JUNCTION (TREFOREST)–LLANTRISANT BRANCH
JUNCTION                                           7 miles 43 chains
*Llantrisant & Taff Vale Junction Railway*

*ACT* : 7 June 1861

*OPENED* : 1 December 1863 *(gds)*, 21 January 1875 *(pass)*

*CLOSED* : 31 March 1952 *(pass)*, 7 September 1963 *(gds)*, Llantrisant Junction–Maesaraul Junction. 28 September 1964 *(min)*, Llantrisant Junction–Cwm Llantwit Colliery Junction. 2 March 1987 *(min)*, Mwyndy Junction–Cwm Llantwit Colliery.

*REMAINS* : Trackbed not yet lifted between Llantrisant Branch Junction–Cwm Llantwit Colliery (SS 067844), and on this section the station buildings at Cross Inn (SS 055831) are noteworthy. North east of the colliery the trackbed, although not continuous, can be traced for most of the way to Llantrisant Junction (SS 089876). The site of Tonteg station remains at SS 096864. The station building at Church Village (SS 086858) is intact, complete with distinctive awning. Underbridges can be found at SS 097869 and SS 074848.

*USES* : A local bus company has built a garage across the line at SS 075852, and a short section south-west of Church Village station is now in a private garden. The station building here is in private hands; so too is Cross Inn, which is used by a light engineering firm.

COMMON BRANCH JUNCTION–LLANTRISANT COMMON JUNCTION
                                                  2 miles 30 chains
*Llantrisant & Taff Vale Junction Railway*

*ACT*: 7 June 1861
*OPENED* : 1 December 1863 *(gds and min)*
*CLOSED* : 1924 *(gds and min)*
*REMAINS* : Trackbed can be traced throughout much of this
   route, except for about ¼-mile westward of the B4270 at ST
   056840, and at ST 044848 (the site of Treferig Junction). The
   stone abutments of a large skew girder bridge remain at ST
   031847, together with abutments and two piers of a small
   girder viaduct at ST 041850. East of the B4270 the line is in a
   deep overgrown cutting and the divergence to form the triangle
   of Common Branch Junction is difficult to follow.
*USES* : A short section of trackbed has been absorbed into the
   site of the Royal Mint (ST 036849).

TREFERIG BRANCH                                   2 miles 56 chains
*Treferig Valley Railway* (later *Taff Vale Railway*)
*ACT*: 21 July 1879
*OPENED* : April 1883 *(gds and min)*
*CLOSED* : 1924 *(gds and min)*
*REMAINS* : A short length of trackbed curving northwards near
   ST 043850. At ST 045863 once existed a bridge—only the
   hump in the road now marks its site. To the north and below
   the road level, part of the parapet is visible. The trackbed itself
   is barely discernible as it runs through the woods here. At ST
   034875 a bridge has once again been filled in, but here stone
   piers are visible on either side of the road. To the south, woods
   again obscure the trackbed, but northwards it has been cleared
   for a short way.
*USES* : The site of Treferig Junction at ST 044848 is now
   occupied by a small factory.

COMMON BRANCH JUNCTION–WATERHALL JUNCTION (TVR)
                                                  7 miles 12 chains
*Llantrisant & Taff Vale Junction Railway*
*ACT*: 7 June 1861
*OPENED* : 11 September 1886 *(gds and min)*
*CLOSED* : 28 September 1964 *(gds and min)*, Waterhall Junction–
   Creigiau Quarry. 31 January 1978 *(min)*, Creigiau Quarry–
   Common Branch Junction.
*REMAINS* : Apart from where the M4 crosses, the trackbed can
   be easily followed for most of the route of this branch. A tall
   sandstone bridge stands at ST 057832. Waterhall Junction (ST
   144783) is best viewed from the road bridge about 100yds to
   the south.
*USES* : The M4 has claimed a length of trackbed at ST 099799.

LLANTRISANT—ABERTHAW                          11 miles 78 chains
*Cowbridge Railway, Cowbridge & Aberthaw Railway*
*ACTS* : 29 July 1862 (Cowbridge Railway), 12 August 1889
   (Cowbridge & Aberthaw Railway)
*OPENED* : February 1865 *(gds)*, 18 September 1865 *(pass)*,
   Llantrisant–Cowbridge. 1 October 1892 *(pass and gds)*, Cow-
   bridge–Aberthaw.
*CLOSED* : 5 May 1930 *(pass)*, 1 November 1932 *(gds)*, Cow-
   bridge–Aberthaw. 26 November 1951 *(pass)*, 1 February 1965
   *(gds)*, Llantrisant–Cowbridge. 28 July 1975 *(min)*, Llantrisant–
   Llanharry iron mine.
*REMAINS* : Whilst the trackbed can be found in many places, a
   great deal has been fenced off for farm use. At Llantrisant
   station site (ST 035814) the branch junction can be seen. At
   ST 018806 the line has been cut by a new road parallel to the
   M4. Northwards from here the line lies in a shallow cutting.
   Southwards, before disappearing beneath the M4, is a small
   bridge which carried the original road here. Between here and
   Cowbridge good views of the trackbed can be found at ST
   011775, ST 008772 and ST 007760. In Cowbridge the two
   bridges beneath the B4270, at ST 000745 and ST 001744 are
   intact, although the cuttings beneath them have been filled.
   South of Cowbridge bridges at ST 010727, ST 017721 and ST
   032696 command fine views. Of particular interest are the
   buildings of St Mary Church Road and St Athan Road stations
   at ST 019717 and ST 031678 respectively. The bridge
   abutments immediately south of the latter are well preserved.
   An embankment continues south, pierced by a single-arch
   stone bridge, before disappearing beneath the cement factory.
   The most southerly remains are a stone underbridge at ST
   034666, beyond the cement factory, while at ST 037663 it is
   just possible to discern the continuation of this branch at a low
   level, beyond its terminus, to the foreshore.
*USES* : Much of the land is now used for farming. Ystradowen
   station site is now a saw mill (ST 013776). Between the
   Cowbridge by-pass (A48) and the B4270 the sites of both
   Cowbridge stations have been obliterated by housing developments. The station buildings at St Mary Church Road and St
   Athan Road are in private use. The Aberthaw & Bristol
   Channel Portland Cement Company Limited occupies the
   railway near ST 032675.

## PORT TALBOT TO SWANSEA

This region once contained the earliest recorded railway in South Wales—a wooden wagonway at Neath—dating from about 1695. Some 50 years later tramways were known to be in existence in the Taibach area of Port Talbot, some time before the better known developments in north-east Glamorgan and north-west Monmouthshire. The most outstanding reminder of these early days of rail transport can be found at Pontrhydyfen, where a little to the east of the Port Talbot Railway viaduct stands a stone viaduct dating from about 1824, that once carried an early tramway. The group of valleys between the Neath and Llynfi rivers, which focus on Port Talbot unlike those to the east, have lost all of their rail connections. The communities here never developed to the size of their neighbours in the surrounding valleys, and the loss of all rail links has left them lonely and isolated, particularly above Pontrhydyfen.

PORT TALBOT (CENTRAL)–PONTYRHYLL JUNCTION    14 miles 1 chain
*Port Talbot Railway & Dock Company*
*ACT*: 31 July 1894
*OPENED* : 1 September 1897 *(gds)*, Port Talbot (Central)–Lletty Brongu. 14 February 1898 *(gds)*, Lletty Brongu–Pontyrhyll Junction. 14 February 1898 *(pass)*, Port Talbot (Central)–Pontyrhyll Junction.
*CLOSED* : 12 September 1932 *(pass)*, Maesteg (Neath Road)–Pontyrhyll. 11 September 1933 *(pass)*, Port Talbot (Central)–Maesteg (Neath Road). 1 February 1960 *(gds)*, Port Talbot (Central)–Duffryn Junction. 9 May 1960 *(gds and min)*, Cwmdu–Pontyrhyll Junction. 31 August 1964 *(gds and min)*, Duffryn Junction–Cwmdu (the section Maesteg–Cwmdu transferred to the NCB).
*REMAINS* : Port Talbot Central station platforms can be found alongside a cinema at SS 768896. Little of the trackbed to Tonygroes East Junction remains, except a short length of embankment at SS 771898. From SS 780897 the trackbed can be traced almost continuously to Pontyrhyll. A twin-arched brick bridge at SS 796901 is noteworthy, built on a sharp skew. There is a fine view to the south from the B4282 at about SS 805920, where about a mile of tall embankment, on a rising gradient, can be traced to past the site of Bryn station (SS 819920). Cwmcerwyn tunnel lies a little further east. Over-bridge at SS 852916. At SS 874893 stands a large, gracefully proportioned red brick viaduct, which is well worth seeing.
*USES* : The approaches to Central Station are occupied by a

GPO building. The nearby embankment (mentioned above) at SS 771898 is used as a spectator embankment for a local football club. From near the site of Tonygroes East Junction and for about 400yds running east the line is beneath the M4. The route near Duffryn Junction has been built upon. In the lower Duffryn valley the trackbed is used as a bridle path by a local riding school.

TONYGROES EAST JUNCTION–ABERAVON TOWN                    46 chains
*Port Talbot Railway & Dock Company*
*ACT* : 7 August 1896
*OPENED* : 17 January 1898 *(gds)*
*CLOSED* : 1 February 1960 *(gds)*
*REMAINS* : One has to look carefully for the little that is left. Tonygroes Junction lies beneath the M4 at SS 773898, and at first sight this road appears to follow the line of the railway. However at SS 772902 the trackbed can be seen for a short distance, identifiable as a grass bank cut by the abutments of two bridges.
*USES* : Tonygroes East Junction—beneath the M4. South of the motorway all railway-owned land (including that of the R&SB) has been bought by the local council, and is being redeveloped.

TONYGROES NORTH JUNCTION–TONMAWR JUNCTION 5 miles 74 chains
*Port Talbot Railway & Dock Company*
*ACT* : 7 August 1896
*OPENED* : 14 November 1898 *(gds and min)*. Date unknown *(pass)*
*CLOSED* : February 1927 *(gds)*, 22 September 1930 *(pass)*, Tonygroes North Junction–Tonmawr Junction. 9 May 1954 *(min)*, Tonygroes North Junction—3 miles 25 chains north of this point (remainder of line connected to Rhondda & Swansea Bay line at Oakwood Ground Frame). 2 November 1964 *(min)*, Oakwood Ground Frame–Tonmawr Junction.
*REMAINS* : The trackbed of this line can be easily followed up the Afan and Pelena valleys to Tonmawr. The outstanding feature of the line is the magnificent, lofty, red brick viaduct at Pontrhydyfen (SS 794942). A little to the east is a stone viaduct, which dates from 1824, and which was used by a tramway. The empty site of Tonmawr Junction is of interest, for its sheer size dominates the valley and divides the village. The site of Tonygroes North Junction was at SS 772903 running off the only extant length of the Tonygroes East

Junction–Aberavon Town section of the PTR. (Only a barely discernible trace remains.)

*USES* : The trackbed immediately north of Tonygroes North Junction has been used for road improvements, which have effectively removed any traces of this junction.

DUFFRYN JUNCTION–COPPER WORKS JUNCTION            75 chains
*Port Talbot Railway & Dock Company*
*ACT* : 31 July 1894
*OPENED* : 17 January 1898 *(gds and min)*
*CLOSED* : 6 February 1967 *(gds and min)*
*REMAINS* : These only exist south of the South Wales main line. A high embankment with red brick viaduct and retaining walls runs southwards around the blast furnaces of the British Steel Corporation's Port Talbot works. It gradually descends to dockside level. Connections from the main line rise to this embankment from north and south. (The former on a viaduct.)
*USES* : A housing estate has been built on the site of Duffryn Junction and the nearby Duffryn Yard locomotive shed.

BRITON FERRY–GLYNCORRWG                    12 miles 19 chains
*South Wales Mineral Railway*
*ACT* : 15 August 1853
*OPENED* : 1 September 1861 *(gds and min)*, Briton Ferry–Tonmawr Tunnel. 10 March 1863 *(gds and min)*, Tonmawr Tunnel–Glyncorrwg. 28 March 1918 *(pass)*, Cymmer Corrwg–Glyncorrwg.
*CLOSED* : 1 June 1910 *(gds and min)*, Briton Ferry–Top of incline. 1950 *(gds and min)* Top of incline–Tonmawr Junction. 13 July 1947 *(gds and min)*, Tonmawr tunnel–Abercregan Sidings. 1 May 1961 *(gds and min)*, Abercregan Sidings–Cymmer Junction. 30 August 1965 *(gds)*, 1970 *(min)*, Cymmer Junction–Glyncorrwg. 2 November 1964 *(min)*, Tonmawr Junction–Tonmawr Tunnel. 22 September 1930 *(pass)*, Cymmer Corrwg–Glyncorrwg.
*REMAINS* : The incline at Briton Ferry can be traced in part. The junction with the main line has disappeared; only a stone abutment of an overbridge can now be seen at SS 743949. The incline can be seen at SS 748949 and SS 752951. At the latter point is a stone underbridge. Trackbed can be traced from just west of the B4287 at SS 781958, to Tonmawr Junction. Beyond here the line can be seen crossing the Pelena river at SS 809961 on a stone bridge. Just before here the branch to Whitworth Colliery swings north and can be followed up to the old workings. Beyond the bridge the shallow cutting was once

much deeper, and beneath, now lies the western entrance of Pelena tunnel, which carried the SWMR to the Afan valley. The line runs on a shelf on the northern side of this valley and is difficult to trace until near Abercregan, SS 847965. After rounding the hillside into the Corrwg valley, the trackbed can be traced northwards to Glyncorrwg.

*USES* : At Briton Ferry the original junction site has been levelled and used in the track re-alignment carried out by the GWR in the 1930s. The lower part of the incline east of SS 748949 is incorporated as a pathway in a park. Landscaping has obliterated a short section in the Pelena valley between Tonmawr Junction and the river crossing.

SWANSEA (RIVERSIDE)–TREHERBERT (R&SB JUNCTION)

25 miles 13 chains

*Rhondda & Swansea Bay Railway*

*ACT* : 10 August 1882

*OPENED* : 2 November 1885 *(pass and gds)*, Aberavon–Cymmer (Afan). 2 June 1890 *(pass and gds)*, Cymmer (Afan)–Blaengwynfi. 2 July 1890 *(pass and gds)*, Blaengwynfi–Blaen Rhondda. 14 July 1890 *(pass and gds)*, Blaen Rhondda–Treherbert (R&SB Junction). 1891 *(gds)*, Aberavon–Port Talbot Dock. 30 December 1893 *(gds)*, Aberavon–Briton Ferry. 14 December 1894 *(gds)*, Briton Ferry–Danygraig, and Neath Canal Side branch. 14 March 1895 *(pass)*, Aberavon–Danygraig, and Neath Canal Side branch. 7 May 1899 *(pass and gds)*, Danygraig–Swansea (Riverside). 13 June 1960 *(pass and gds)*, new connecting spurs to and from ex-GWR line between Cymmer (Afan) and Blaengwynfi.

*CLOSED* : 11 September 1933 *(pass)*, Jersey Marine–Swansea (Riverside). 16 September 1935 *(pass)*, Briton Ferry (East)–Jersey Marine, and Neath Canal Side branch. 13 June 1960 *(pass and gds)*, Cymmer (Afan)–Blaengwynfi (via R&SB tracks, the service between these points continued via the GWR tracks over the new connecting spurs). 3 December 1962 *(pass)*, Briton Ferry–Cymmer (Afan). (Passenger services to Treherbert continued from Bridgend.) 6 September 1965 *(gds)*, Neath Canal Side branch. 26 February 1968 *(pass and gds)* Cymmer (Afan)–Treherbert (R&SB Junction). (This followed the closure of the Rhondda tunnel on this date. The service was replaced by buses which ran until 14 December 1970, the official closure date.) 2 November 1964 *(gds and min)*, Duffryn Rhondda–Briton Ferry (East). 22 January 1970 *(min)*, Cymmer-Duffryn Rhondda.

*REMAINS* : West of Briton Ferry, where the separate tracks of the R&SB have been absorbed into the rail access to Swansea Docks, or have been re-aligned for road improvements, two reminders of the old company remain. At Danygraig, SS 694932, the fire damaged stone-built locomotive shed still stands, and at the junction of the Swansea Avoiding line, SS 742956, the down line of that system passes beneath the South Wales Main Line via an R&SB underbridge, built to carry its line beneath that of the GWR. From SS 767904 the trackbed can be followed up the Afan valley to just west of Abergwynfi. The earthworks and bridge abutments in the Pontrhydyfen area are noteworthy (SS 797942). An R&SB bridge crosses the river at SS 865960, and at SS 871961 is a short tunnel. Only the northern portal of the Rhondda tunnel can now be reached, at SS 916987, by walking along the trackbed from Blaen Rhondda. The low girder viaduct over the Rhondda Fawr at SS 934986 still stands intact, as do the other bridges on this section and the nearby platforms of Blaen Rhondda station. The trackbed can be traced to the site of the once extensive Rhondda & Swansea Bay Junction with the Taff Vale Railway.

USES : The one-time locomotive shed at Danygraig is now in industrial use. At Baglan a short realigned section is incorporated into the sidings serving the BP chemical plant. Behind the Sandfields estate at Aberavon about a mile of railway has been replaced by a road. In Port Talbot all trace south of the motorway has been obliterated by urban redevelopment, or its associated road network. Land reclamation has removed all traces in the upper Afan valley from a point just to the west of Blaengwynfi, including the adjacent GWR tracks, and the southern portal of the Rhondda tunnel. The inscribed stone from this portal is now set into a wall at the Afan Argoed Country Park. The site of Cynonville halt is a picnic area.

NANTYFFYLLON–ABERGWYNFI    5 miles 38 chains
*Llynfi & Ogmore Railway*
ACTS : 21 July 1873 (Llynfi & Ogmore Railway)
OPENED : 1 July 1878 *(gds and min)*, Nantyffyllon–Abergwynfi (and connection to SWMR, Cymmer Tunnel Junction–Cymmer Junction SWMR). 16 July 1880 *(pass)*, Nantyffyllon–Cymmer (General). 22 March 1886 *(pass)*, Cymmer (General)–Abergwynfi. 13 June 1960 *(pass and gds)*, new connecting spurs to and from R&SB line between Cymmer (General) and Abergwynfi.
CLOSED : 13 June 1960 *(pass)*, 27 May 1963 *(gds)*, Cymmer (General)–Abergwynfi (services continued via Cymmer (Afan)

and Blaengwynfi, over the new connections, using R&SB stations, but GWR tracks). 7 June 1965 *(gds)*, 22 June 1970 *(pass)*, Nantyffyllon–Cymmer (Afan). (School trains continued until 15 July 1970, the official closure date.)

REMAINS : Only the southern end of Cymmer Tunnel can be found at SS 855944. In the Afan valley the platforms of Cymmer (General) station still remain at SS 859961. The trackbed can be traced to just west of Abergwynfi. Of note is the lattice girder viaduct at SS 857961, which carried the line to the SWMR in the Corrwg valley.

USES : Land reclamation has claimed the line (and the adjacent R&SB line) in the Abergwynfi/Blaengwynfi area at the head of the Afan valley. The northern tunnel entrance at Cymmer, and a short section northwards now buried for road improvements.

## SWANSEA TO LLANELLY

Swansea and surrounding district was where three national railway companies competed for the valuable traffic of this rich industrial area, where if the GWR had been somewhat more wide awake in the 1860s and 1870s it could have had all this traffic for itself. It did succeed in impressing itself upon the travelling public with the imposing facade of High Street station, fronting its neat concourse and long gracefully-canopied curving platforms. This was a delightful contrast to the gloomy LNWR Victoria station, with its all-over roof supported on cast-iron columns, and the exposed MR St Thomas station with its solitary open platform.

SWANSEA (VICTORIA)–PONTARDULAIS 12½ miles
*Llanelly Railway & Dock Company* (later *London & North Western Railway*)

ACTS : 1 August 1861 (Llanelly Railway), 1 July 1871 (London & North Western Railway)

OPENED : January 1866 *(gds)*, 14 December 1867 *(pas.)*, Pontardulais–Swansea (Victoria)

CLOSED : 15 June 1964 *(pass)*, Pontardulais–Swansea (Victoria) 4 October 1965 *(gds)*, Gorseinon–Swansea (Victoria). 4 October 1965 *(gds)*, 26 September 1974 *(min)*, Pontardulais–1¾mp. 17 December 1984 *(min)*, 2mp–Gorseinon. 8 October 1986 *(min)*, 1¾mp–2mp (together with the new chord built from The Swansea Avoiding Line (GWR), opened 22 September 1974, prior to closure of LNWR line from Pontardulais. The new chord replaced that of the original line from Grovesend Colliery Loop Junction, opened c 1913.)

*REMAINS* : Bridge abutments at SS 627915 and SS 619907 are the only remains alongside Swansea Bay. Trackbed can be followed between the bridges at SS 597924 (Killay station site) and SS 594937 (Dunvant station site). Further north remains include the abutments of the bridge over the South Wales main line (SS 593965), and road bridges at SS 594977 and SN 595017. At Pontardulais station (SN 588040) the junction can be traced and the course of the line behind the platform.

*USES* : Victoria station is now the site of the Swansea Leisure Centre, and except for a short length near the leisure centre, the coastal section is now used for recreation, walking and golf. Gowerton junction is now a car park. The goods shed at Pontardulais is used by the local council for heavy machinery storage.

GOWERTON–LLANMORLAIS 4¾ miles
*Llanelly Railway & Dock Company* (later *London & North Western Railway*)
*ACTS* : 1 August 1861 (Llanelly Railway), 1 July 1871 (London & North Western Railway)
*OPENED* : January 1866 *(gds)*, 14 December 1867 *(pass)*, Gowerton–Penclawdd. 1877 *(gds and pass)*, Gowerton–Llanmorlais
*CLOSED* : 5 January 1931 *(pass)*, 2 September 1957 *(gds)*, Gowerton–Llanmorlais
*REMAINS* : The route can be followed from the junction at the site of Gowerton station (LNWR) at SS 592964 to Penclawdd station site, where a platform face remains adjacent to the B4295 (SS 546958). Beyond, only a road bridge parapet remains at SS 541958, together with a footbridge a little to the east. Llanmorlais station buildings stand at SS 533946.
*USES* : From Gowerton station (LNWR) to the B4296 at SS 588966 each end of the cutting is now a municipal car park, linked by a footpath. West of Penclawdd station site private development occupies most of the course to Llanmorlais, where the station is now a private house.

SWANSEA (ST THOMAS)–BRYNAMMAN, VIA SIX PIT JUNCTION
18 miles 63 chains
*Swansea Vale Railway* (later *Midland Railway*)
*ACTS* : 15 June 1855, 22 July 1861 (Swansea Vale Railway); 1 July 1874 (Midland Railway)
*OPENED* : Before 1850 *(gds)* lower 8 miles, *circa* 1859 *(gds)* extension to Ynyscedwn. 1 January 1864 *(gds)* Ystalyfera–Brynamman. 1868 *(pass)* Swansea–Brynamman

*CLOSED* : 25 September 1950 *(pass)*, Swansea (St Thomas)–Brynamman (East). The passenger service betwen Upper Bank and Glais ran via Morriston (East)—see next section. 28 September 1964 *(gds)*, Gurnos–Brynamman (East). 28 September 1964 *(min)*, Blaencwm colliery (lower Cwm Twrch)–Brynamman (East). 12 July 1965 *(gds)*, Swansea–Gurnos. 30 April 1968 *(min)*, Six Pit Junction–Gurnos. 24 May 1983 *(min)*, Swansea Eastern Depot–Upper Bank Junction.

*REMAINS* : Trackbed can be traced from near St Thomas station to Upper Bank Junction. To the east of SS 683967 it is just possible to discern the formation running from Swansea Valley Junction on the main line. Road bridges remain at SS 689975 and SN 714022, whilst a fine brick bridge with a central girder span carries the Swansea Avoiding Line over the branch at SS 695979. Trackbed can be traced in the vicinity of these bridges, and then with some difficulty north of Pontardawe where it is in thick woodland until just before Ynisygeinon Junction (SN 765075), where it runs on an embankment. Bridge abutments at SN 765083 and SN 761107 mark the crossing of the Tawe and Afon Twrch respectively. From SN 743134 the trackbed runs westward to Brynamman.

*USES* : Housing estate at SS 695985. The track at SN 765085 incorporated into a new road, beyond which the track has been landscaped at the entrance to the Cwm Twrch valley. At SN 756110 the track forms the eastbound lane of a dual carriageway.

UPPER BANK JUNCTION–GLAIS JUNCTION (VIA MORRISTON EAST)

4 miles 65 chains

*Swansea Vale Railway* (later *Midland Railway*)

*ACT* : 17 June 1867

*OPENED* : Circa 1869 *(gds)*, 1 March 1875 *(pass)*

*CLOSED* : 25 September 1950 *(pass)*, Upper Bank Junction–Glais Junction (via Morriston (East)). 12 September 1965 *(gds and min)*, Morriston (East)–Clydach on Tawe South. 4 October 1965 *(gds)*, Upper Bank Junction–Morriston (East). 30 April 1968 *(min)*, Clydach on Tawe South–Glais Junction. 24 May 1983 *(min)*, Upper Bank Junction–Morriston (East).

*REMAINS* : Station site at Morriston (East), SS 674977. Near SS 675987 the trackbed can be traced until it disappears beneath a motorway junction, beyond the roundabout it is alongside but below the level of the A4067.

YNISYGEINON JUNCTION–COLBREN JUNCTION                6¾ miles
*Swansea Vale & Neath & Brecon Junction Railway*

*ACT* : 29 July 1864
*OPENED* : 26 July 1869
*CLOSED* : 20 February 1967 *(gds and min)*, Ynisygeinon Junction–Abercrave International Colliery Sidings. 12 October 1967 *(gds and min)*, Abercrave International Colliery Sidings–Colbren Junction. 12 September 1932 *(pass)*, Ynisygeinon Junction–Colbren Junction.
*REMAINS* : A fine stone bridge stands alongside the main road at SN 836121. At Colbren Junction (SN 851115) only the grass-covered station platforms remain.

CLYDACH ON TAWE (NORTH)–TREBANOS     1 mile 75 chains
*Great Western Railway*
*ACT* : 18 August 1911
*OPENED* : 3 August 1923 *(min only)*, Clydach on Tawe North–Daren Colliery (Trebanos)
*CLOSED* : 1 February 1965 *(min only)*, Clydach on Tawe North–Daren Colliery (Trebanos)
*REMAINS* : Bridge abutments at SN 710027
*USES* : Where the branch ran through Clydach, north of the A4067, housing developments have taken place.

HAFOD JUNCTION–FELIN FRAN JUNCTION (WEST)    3 miles 21 chains
*Great Western Railway*
*ACT* : 25 July 1872; 15 August 1904
*OPENED* : 9 May 1881 *(pass and gds)*, Hafod Junction–Morriston (West). 8 May 1914 *(pass and gds)*, Morriston (West)–Felin Fran Junction (West)
*CLOSED* : 11 June 1956 *(pass)*, 4 October 1965 *(gds)*, Hafod Junction–Felin. Fran Junction (West). (The line remained open to diverted Sunday passenger traffic until 9 September 1963.)
*REMAINS* : The high-level Hafod Junction can be seen where the main line crosses the A4067 at SS 660952, it is high up at the viaduct level to the east of the road. Morriston West station platforms and building (south of A48) still stand at SS 672979. The abutments of the viaduct and a small portion of the embankment where the branch crossed the LMS Swansea valley line and ran up to the main line at Felin Fran West remain at SS 676990.

THE SWANSEA HIGH LEVEL LINES (EAST DOCK AND NORTH DOCK TO SOUTH DOCK)    Aggregate mileage 1 mile 10 chains
*South Wales Railway, Vale of Neath Railway*
*ACTS* : 27 July 1846 (South Wales Railway); 10 August 1857,

6 August 1861 (Vale of Neath Railway)

OPENED : June 1852 *(gds and min)*, North Dock Junction–North Dock. (Extended in September 1859.) 23 September 1859 *(gds and min)*, North Dock–South Dock. 15 July 1863 *(min)*, 1 August 1863 *(pass)*, 24 August 1863 *(gds)*, East Dock–Wind Street Junction.

CLOSED : March 1873 *(pass)*, East Dock–Wind Street. 15 June 1964 *(gds and min)*, Swansea East Dock–Wind Street (Burrows Lodge) Junction. 4 October 1965 *(gds and min)*, Wind Street (Burrows Lodge) Junction–Victoria No 2–South Dock. 1 November 1965 *(gds and min)*, North Dock Junction–Wind Street (Burrows Lodge) Junction.

REMAINS : The viaducts carrying these lines remain in two isolated sections; at SS 661932, and at SS 658925.

USES : Where the viaducts have been levelled the land is used for car parks, road widening or light industry. The section at SS 658925 is incorporated into the Swansea Leisure Centre.

DAFEN BRANCH                                    2 miles 53 chains
*Llanelly Railroad & Dock Company*
ACT : 19 June 1828
OPENED : 1833 *(min)*, Llanelly Dock–Dafen, 20 April 1903 *(min)*, 63 chain extension.
CLOSED : 4 March 1963 *(min and gds)*
REMAINS : Apart from a short stretch the trackbed of this branch, north of the South Wales main line, can be traced from SS 515993 to SN 531011.
USES : Apart from a rugby football ground at SS 521998, and a short length near the main line crossing, the trackbed is used as a public footpath. At SN 525005 and SN 531011 it has been landscaped and seats set up for the public.

PEMBREY–LLANELLY (SANDY JUNCTION)
*Burry Port & Gwendraeth Valley Railway*
ACT : 30 April 1866
OPENED : 28 July 1891 *(gds and min)*. Burry Port–Sandy Junction
CLOSED : 2 August 1967 *(gds and min)*. Burry Port–Sandy Junction (The branch connection at Pembrey had been taken out of use 22 December 1963.)
REMAINS : Site of Sandy Junction at SN 498005. Trackbed adjacent to A484 (to the south and below road level) between SN 483008 and SN 476009. Site of junction with main line at SN 453007.
USES : A council depot occupies a site at SN 474009.

BURRY PORT–KIDWELLY JUNCTION                4 miles 74 chains
*Bury Port & Gwendraeth Valley Railway*
*ACT* : 30 April 1866
*OPENED* : July 1869 *(min and gds)*, 2 August 1900 *(pass)*, Burry
    Port–Kidwelly Junction.
*CLOSED* : 21 September 1953 *(pass)*, 7 June 1965 *(gds)*, Burry
    Port–Kidwelly Junction. 17 September 1983 *(min)*, Burry
    Port–Kidwelly Junction.
*REMAINS* : Trackbed from near Burry Port & Pembrey station
    to Kidwelly Junction. Underbridge on South Wales main line
    at SN 442007. Overbridges at SN 437009 and SN 428012.
    Gwendraeth Fawr crossed at SN 428053.

TRIMSARAN JUNCTION–TRIMSARAN COLLIERY        2 miles (approx)
*Burry Port & Gwendraeth Valley Railway*
*ACT* : 30 April 1866
*OPENED* : June 1873 *(gds and min)*, Trimsaran Junction–
    Trimsaran Colliery.
*CLOSED* : circa 1957 *(gds and min)*, Trimsaran Junction–
    Trimsaran Colliery.
*REMAINS* : None.

KIDWELLY JUNCTION–MYNYDD Y GARREG          2 miles 10 chains
*Gwendraeth Valley Railway*
*ACT* : 30 July 1866
*OPENED* : 1871 *(gds and min)*, Kidwelly Junction–Mynydd y
    Garreg
*CLOSED* : 28 August 1960 *(gds and min)*, Kidwelly Junction–
    Mynydd y Garreg. (Official date, traffic ceased February
    1959.)
*REMAINS* : Short length of embankment north of A484 at SN
    408063. Cutting beneath bridge on B4308 (SN 413065).
    Trackbed visible at SN 424076, north and south of minor road,
    and about ¼-mile south of SN 426081.

KIDWELLY HARBOUR-COED BACH WASHERY (AND KIDWELLY
JUNCTION–TYCOCH JUNCTION)              Aggregate mileage 2 miles
*Burry Port & Gwendraeth Valley Railway*, and *Gwendraeth Valley
Railway*.
*ACTS* : 30 April 1866 (Burry Port & Gwendraeth Valley
    Railway); 30 July 1866 (Gwendraeth Valley Railway)
*OPENED* : June 1873
*CLOSED* : 1934 *(gds and min)*, Kidwelly Harbour–Tycoch
    Junction. 26 October 1964 *(gds and min)*, Kidwelly Junction–
    Coed Bach Washery.

*RE-OPENED* : 19 September 1983 *(min)*, Kidwelly Junction–
Coedbach Washery.

*REMAINS* : Only the remains of the canal basin and the
riverside quay exist south of the main line (SN 398065). A
bridge on the A484 crosses a shallow cutting at SN 408061.

SWANSEA & MUMBLES RAILWAY                              7½ miles
*Oystermouth Railway Company*
*ACTS* : 29 June 1804 (Oystermouth Railway), 26 August 1889
(Mumbles Railway & Pier Company), 26 July 1893 (Swansea
& Mumbles Railway).

*OPENED* : April 1806 *(gds)*, 25 March 1807 *(pass)* Swansea–
Oystermouth. 6 May 1893 *(pass)* Oystermouth–Southend. 10
May 1898 *(pass)* Southend–Mumbles Pier.

*CLOSED* : 11 October 1959 *(pass)* Southend–Mumbles Pier. 5
January 1960 *(pass)* Swansea (Rutland Street)–Southend. 1962
*(gds)* Strand–Victoria Road (Rutland Street). The section from
the Swansea Canal to Victoria Road, and the Clyne valley
branch (both goods only) closed about the turn of the century.

*USES* : The entire length alongside Swansea Bay is now owned
by the local council. It is used for public amenities eg walking
and golf (as is the adjacent LNWR line). Some sections have
been incorporated into the main road where it has been
widened.

# CARMARTHEN

The closures of the last two decades struck the old counties of
Cardiganshire, Carmarthenshire and Pembrokeshire extremely
hard. Some 140 miles of disused trackbed now wend their way
across hills and along delightful river valleys. In most cases,
although not specifically mentioned in the details of *Remains* that
follow, many miles can still be walked. Unlike the forgotten lines
to the east they have not yet been claimed for roads, nor as in the
Breconshire and Herefordshire border region have they been
totally re-absorbed into agricultural usage.

CARMARTHEN–NEWCASTLE EMLYN                   17 miles 53 chains
*Carmarthen & Cardigan Railway, Great Western Railway*
*ACTS* : 7 August 1854 (Carmarthen & Cardigan Railway), 22
August 1881 (purchased by Great Western Railway)

*OPENED* : 3 September 1860 *(pass and gds)*, Carmarthen Town–
Conwil. 28 March 1864 *(pass and gds)*, Conwil–Pencader. 3
June 1864 *(pass and gds)*, Pencader–Llandyssul. 1 July 1895
*(pass and gds)*, Llandyssul–Newcastle Emlyn.

*CLOSED* : 15 September 1952 *(pass)*, Pencader Junction–
Newcastle Emlyn. 28 September 1973 *(gds)*, Carmarthen
Town–Newcastle Emlyn. 22 February 1965 *(pass)* Carmarthen
Town–Pencader Junction.
(*Note* : Traffic ceased 31 December 1861, and recommenced
12 August 1862.)
*REMAINS* : Only two railway buildings remain, the station
house at Llanpumpsaint, and the goods shed at Newcastle
Emlyn. Bridges remain at SN 430216 and SN 415296 (both
stone); also at SN 411400, SN 408402, and SN 357407 (girder).
The river bridge still stands at SN 334409.
*USES* : Between Bronwydd Arms (SN 417238) and Llwyfan
Cerrig used by the Gwili Railway Company, which owns the
trackbed north to Llanpumpsaint. Llanpumpsaint station yard
is used by a farmers' co-operative; those at Llandyssul and
Newcastle Emlyn are used as coal depots.

PENCADER JUNCTION–ABERYSTWYTH                41 miles 25 chains
*Manchester & Milford Railway*
*ACTS* : 23 July 1860 and 5 July 1865 (Manchester & Milford
Railway), 2 June 1911 (absorbed by Great Western Railway)
*OPENED :* 1 January 1866 *(pass and gds)*, Pencader–Lampeter. 1
September 1866 *(pass and gds)*, Lampeter–Strata Florida. 12
August 1867 *(pass and gds)*, Strata Florida–Aberystwyth.
*CLOSED* : 14 December 1964 *(pass)*, 2 December 1963 *(gds)*,
Caradoc Falls Halt–Aberystwyth. 22 February 1965 *(pass)*,
Pencader Junction–Strata Florida. 16 March 1964 *(gds)*, Pont
Llanio–Strata Florida. 1969 *(gds)*, Aberayron Junction–Pont
Llanio. 30 September 1973 *(gds)*, Pencader Junction–
Aberayron Junction.
*REMAINS* : Only the station buildings and goods sheds at
Llanybyther (SN 522441) and Lampeter (SN 582484) remain.
Stone bridges stand at SN 475409, SN 478412, SN 552459, SN
694695 and SN 665728; girder bridges at SN 447385 and SN
582476; stone abutments only stand at SN 506425, SN 582475,
SN 664735 and SN 591780.
*USES* : Llanybyther station site has a multiplicity of uses. The
station building houses the local rugby club, the opposite
platform is used to store new farm machinery, whilst the goods
shed is a warehouse. Lampeter station site has been leased to
the University of Wales (St David's University College).
Strata Florida station site (SN 711671) is now a holiday
caravan site, the trackbed to the south being incorporated as a
footpath through a nature reserve. Trawscoed station site SN
666726 houses a coal depot. At Aberystwyth station (SN

585816) the bay platform used by Carmarthen trains is now used by the Vale of Rheidol narrow gauge line, whilst the curve to the south has been incorporated into the local cattle market.

LAMPETER–ABERAYRON                                    12 miles 14 chains
*Lampeter, Aberayron & Newquay Light Railway*
*LIGHT RAILWAY ORDER* : October 1906
*OPENED* : 10 April 1911 *(gds)*, 12 May 1911 *(pass)*, Aberayron Junction–Aberayron.
*CLOSED* : 7 May 1951 *(pass)*, Aberayron Junction–Aberayron. 5 April 1965 *(gds)*, Green Grove Siding–Aberayron. 30 September 1973 *(gds)*, Aberayron Junction–Green Grove Siding.
*REMAINS* : Platform at Talsarn Halt (SN 543547), rails embedded in road at adjacent level-crossing site. A further set of rails are embedded at the crossing at SN 531556. River bridge at SN 460623.
*USES* : Sections of trackbed north of Cilau-Ayron are used as footpaths. Aberayron station site (SN 459623) re-developed as offices of the Welsh National Water Development Authority. The nearby river bridge is used as road access to a builders' merchant.

ABERGWILI JUNCTION–LLANDILO                           13 miles 20 chains
*Llanelly Railway & Dock Company* (later *London & North Western Railway*)
*ACTS* : 1 August 1861 (Llanelly Railway), 1 July 1871 (absorption by London & North Western Railway)
*OPENED* : November 1864 *(gds)*, 1 June 1865 *(pass)*, Abergwili Junction–Llandilo
*CLOSED* : 9 September 1963 *(pass and gds)*, Abergwili Junction–Llandilo.
*REMAINS* : The stone station buildings at Abergwili (SN 436212), Nantgaredig (SN 494207), Llanarthney (SN 534205), Drysllwyn (SN 554198) and Golden Grove (SN 590211) all remain intact. At Golden Grove stands a LNWR starter signal. A small tunnel runs under the A40 at SN 445211. A river bridge remains at SN 516207.
*USES* : All the stations noted are now private houses. The goods yard at Nantgaredig is used by a farmers' co-operative.

CARDIGAN JUNCTION–CARDIGAN                            25 miles 18 chains
*Whitland & Cardigan Railway* (originally *Whitland & Taf Vale Railway*)

*ACTS* : 12 July 1869 (Whitland & Taf Vale Railway) 1877 (Whitland & Cardigan Railway)

*OPENED* : 24 March 1873 *(gds)*, Cardigan Junction–Glogue. July 1874 *(gds)* Glogue–Crymmych Arms. 12 July 1875 *(pass)*, Cardigan Junction–Crymmych Arms. 1 September 1886 *(pass and gds)*, Crymmych Arms–Cardigan.

*CLOSED* : 10 September 1962 *(pass)*, 27 May 1963 *(gds)*, Cardigan Junction–Cardigan

*REMAINS* : Station buildings remain at all sites except Kilgerran (SN 188429), Glogue (SN 216325), Rhydowen (SN 195285) and Llanfalteg (SN 156200). Bridge abutments remain at Kilgerran and at SN 202427, and the complete bridge at Crymmych Arms station (SN 185338). Level-crossing gates abound. At Boncath (SN 204385), Rhydowen, Llanglydwen (SN 181268) and at SN 164218 both gates remain, whilst at Glogue, Login (SN 167235) and Llanfalteg only one.

*USES* : The station buildings at Crymmych Arms, Llanfyrnach (SN 222312) and Llanglydwen are private houses, all modified to some degree. Login is now a farmhouse, and the station yard the farm yard. Boncath is in the grounds of a private house. Llanglydwen station yard is a coal depot. Cardigan station, goods shed and station yard are used by local engineering and agricultural businesses. The trackbed as far as Kilgerran is a footpath through the Cardigan Wildlife Park.

JOHNSTON–NEYLAND                                    3¾ miles
*South Wales Railway*
*ACT* : 17 June 1852
*OPENED* : 15 April 1856 *(pass and gds)*, Johnston–Neyland
*CLOSED* : 15 June 1964 *(pass and gds)*, Johnston–Neyland
*REMAINS* : Trackbed only for most of the route. It is best seen from the bridge at SM 967060, which commands a view from Neyland station site northwards for about one mile.
*USES* : Station site is now used for light industry.

CLYNDERWEN–LETTERSTON JUNCTION              17 miles 12 chains
*North Pembroke & Fishguard Railway* (later *Great Western Railway*)
*ACTS* : 7 August 1887 (North Pembroke & Fishguard Railway), 12 February 1898 (Great Western Railway)
*1ST OPENING* : 19 September 1876 *(pass and gds)*, Clynderwen-Rosebush.
*1ST CLOSURE* : 31 September 1882 *(pass and gds)*, Clynderwen-Rosebush.
*2ND OPENING* : 14 March 1895 *(gds)*, 11 April 1895 *(pass)*, Clynderwen–Letterston Junction.

*2ND CLOSURE* : 8 January 1917 *(pass and gds)*, Clynderwen–
Letterston Junction.
*3RD OPENING* : 12 July 1920 *(pass and gds)*, Clynderwen–
Rosebush. 14 November 1921 *(pass and gds)* Rosebush–
Puncheston. 9 July 1923 *(pass and gds)*, Puncheston–Letterston
Junction.
*3RD CLOSURE* : 25 October 1937 *(pass)*, Clynderwen–
Letterston Junction. Line closed during 1939–45 War (date
unknown), and area around Maenclochog used for target
practice by RAF and USAF. The section Letterston–Puncheston never reopened.
*4TH OPENING* : During 1939–1945 War (date unknown),
following repairs after use for target practice.
*4TH CLOSURE* : 16 May 1949 *(gds)*, Clynderwen–Letterston
(official date, actually only as far as Puncheston). 1 March
1965 *(gds)*, Letterston Junction–Letterston.
*REMAINS* : Brick overbridge at SN 101205, stone overbridges at
SN 083268, SN 076282 and SN 074291. Onward to Letterston
Junction only stone bridge abutments remain at SN 066299,
SN 008294, SM 995286, SM 981284, SM 941310 and SM
940314. (This latter spanned the A40 and should not be
confused with the Trecwn branch bridge about 100yds further
north.) The wooden station building at Letterston remains, as
does the girder bridge to the north-west (SM 956296 and SM
953298 respectively).
*USES* : Maenclochog station site is a bus park, and Letterston
station is a private house.

SAUNDERSFOOT RAILWAY                    Aggregate mileage 8½ miles
*ACT* : 1 June 1829, and 1842
*OPENED* : 1832 *(min)*, Saundersfoot Harbour–Thomas Chapel
Mines. 1842 *(min)*, Saundersfoot Harbour–Kilgetty Colliery.
1915 *(min)* Thomas Chapel Mines–Reynalton Colliery.
*CLOSED* : Circa April 1930.
*RE-OPENED* : 1935 *(min)*, Saundersfoot Harbour–Broom
Colliery. Circa 1936 *(min)*, Saundersfoot Harbour–Kilgetty
Colliery.
*FINAL CLOSURE* : February 1939 *(min)*, Saundersfoot Harbour
–Kilgetty Colliery. August 1939 *(min)*, Saundersfoot Harbour–
Broom Colliery.
*REMAINS* : Tunnels along the coast north of Saundersfoot,
bridge beneath the A477 at Stepaside (SN 137076). The
harbour offices.
*USES* : The coastal section north to Wiseman's Bridge is a
footpath and uses the original tunnels. The harbour offices are
now a restaurant.

AMOCO JUNCTION–HERBRANSTON OIL REFINERY        1 mile 28 chains
*British Railways (Western Region)*
*ACT* :
*OPENED* : 21 August 1960 *(min)*, Amoco Junction–Herbranston
    Oil Refinery.
*CLOSED* : 11 January 1984 *(min)*, Amoco Junction–Herbranston
    Oil Refinery.
*REMAINS* : Trackbed.

# Bibliography

The following is intended as a guide to those who may wish to study the railways of the region in greater depth. The list while covering the whole of South Wales is not exhaustive. In some of the locally published books railway references are sometimes merely incidental, reflecting the fact that at one time the railway was so much a part of the everyday scene that it was largely taken for granted.

General Books
*A History of British Railways down to the year 1830*, C. F. Dendy Marshall, Oxford Publishing Co
*Bradshaws April 1910 Railway Guide*, David & Charles
*Britain's Joint Stations*, H. C. Casserley, Ian Allan
*British Railway Tunnels*, A. Blower, Ian Allan
*The Canals of South Wales & The Border*, C. Hadfield, David & Charles
*GWR Service Timetable Appendices 1945*, D. Bradford Barton
*GWR Timetable 1902*, Oxford Publishing Co
*GWR Timetable 1932*, Oxford Publishing Co
*GWR Timetable 1947*, Oxford Publishing Co
*History of the Great Western Railway*, (Vols 1 and 2) E. T. McDermott and C. R. Clinker, Ian Allan
*Passengers no more*, G. Daniels & L. A. Dench, Ian Allan
*The Railway Clearing House Handbook of Railway Stations 1904*, Railway Clearing House, David & Charles
*Railway Junction Diagrams 1915*, Railway Clearing House, David & Charles
*Register of closed passenger & goods stations*, C. R. Clinker
*Stone Blocks & Iron Rails*, B. Baxter, David & Charles
*Twixt Rail & Sea*, W. G. Chapman, Patrick Stephens Ltd (originally Great Western Railway Company)
*Welsh Coal Mines*, Dr W. Gerwyn Thomas, National Museum of Wales

Chapter 2
*The Brecon & Merthyr Railway*, D. S. Barrie, Oakwood Press
*The Brecon & Merthyr Railway*, V. J. Parry, Brecon & Radnor Express

*The Cambrian Railways* (2 Vols), Rex Christiansen & R. W. Miller, David & Charles
*Forgotten Railways, North & Mid Wales*, Rex Christiansen, David & Charles
*The History of the Midland Railway*, C. E. Stretton, Methuen & Co
*Midland Railway*, Williams, David & Charles

Chapter 3
*The Great Western Railway in Dean*, H. W. Paar, David & Charles
*Historical Notes on the Railways of S.E. Monmouthshire*, A. J. Pritchard, Oakwood Press

Chapter 4
*Britain's Railways in World War I*, J. A. B. Hamilton, Allen & Unwin
*A History of Ebbw Vale*, A. Gray Jones, Starling Press
*A History of GWR Goods Wagons* (Vol 2), A. G. Atkins, *et al*, David & Charles
'The LNWR in South Wales', W. Jones, *Railway World* April/ June 1957
*Merthyr Historian*, Merthyr Tydfil Historical Society

Chapter 5
'The Alexandra (Newport & South Wales) Dock & Railway', W. Jones, *Railway World* May 1956
*The Early Days of Sirhowy & Tredegar*, O. Jones, Starling Press
'Halts to Caerphilly & Machen', I. L. Wright, *Trains Illustrated*, November 1956
*A History of Rudry*, Rev. J. Guy, Starling Press
*The Sirhowy Valley & Its Railways*, D. S. Barrie & C. E. Lee, Railway Publishing Co Ltd

Chapter 6
*The Barry Railway*, D. S. Barrie, Oakwood Press
*The Rhymney Railway*, D. S. Barrie, Oakwood Press
*The Taff Vale Railway*, D. S. Barrie, Oakwood Press
*Taff Vale Railway Rule Book, 1853*, Taff Vale Railway

Chapter 7
*Gilfach Goch in Cameo* (2 Vols), K. O. Pritchard, Starling Press
*Newton Nottage & Porthcawl*, L. S. Higgins, Gomerian Press

Chapter 8
*Port Talbot Railway & Docks*, A. Havelock Case, Port Talbot Railway Co (1898)

'The Port Talbot & South Wales Mineral Railways', W. Jones *Railway World*, November 1955
'The Rhondda & Swansea Bay Railway', W. Jones, *Railway World*, December 1955

Chapter 9
'The Gwendraeth Valley Railway', J. Bourne, *Trains Illustrated*, November 1952
'The Neath & Brecon and Midland Railways', W. Jones, *Railway World*, March 1956
*Shrewsbury to Swansea*, D. J. Smith, Town & Country Press
*The Story of Swansea & District Villages*, N. L. Thomas, Qualprint (Wales) Ltd Swansea

Chapter 10
*The North Pembroke & Fishguard Railway*, J. P. Morris, Oakwood Press
*The Saundersfoot Railway*, M. R. C. Price, Oakwood Press
*The Teifi Valley Railway*, R. Padfield & B. Burgess, Laidlaw-Burgess, Haverfordwest
*The Whitland & Cardigan Railway*, M. R. C. Price, Oakwood Press

# Index